HOLY WEEK

H O L Y W E E K

**INTERPRETING
THE LESSONS OF
THE CHURCH YEAR**

WALTER WINK

**PROCLAMATION 5
SERIES B**

FORTRESS PRESS MINNEAPOLIS

PROCLAMATION 5
Interpreting the Lessons of the Church Year
Series B, Holy Week

Cover and interior design: Spangler Design Team

Library of Congress Cataloging-in-Publication Data
(Revised for Ser. B, v. 1-4)

Proclamation 5.

   Contents: ser. A. [2] Epiphany / Pheme Perkins —
[etc.] — ser. B. [1] Advent/Christmas / William H.
Willimon — [2] Epiphany / David Rhoads — [3] Lent /
Thomas Hoyt, Jr. — [4] Holy Week / Walter Wink.
   1. Bible—Homiletical use. 2. Bible—Liturgical
lessons, English. I. Perkins, Pheme.
BS534.5.P765 1993   251   92-22973
ISBN 0-8006-4185-X (ser. B, Advent/Christmas)
ISBN 0-8006-4186-8 (ser. B, Epiphany)
ISBN 0-8006-4187-6 (ser. B, Lent)
ISBN 0-8006-4188-4 (ser. B, Holy Week)

Manufactured in the U.S.A.   AF 1-4188

97   96   95   94   93   1   2   3   4   5   6   7   8   9   10

CONTENTS

Introduction

The events of Holy Week are the gospel story at its climax. No other season of the Christian year is so charged with tension, so filled with meaning, so foundational to faith. Sadly, many churches will observe only a few of the days of Holy Week, or, if they do, only a few people may attend. What a lost opportunity! For nowhere else are we exposed to the gospel in such raw and rich intensity. In these eight days we see the drama of Jesus' last days: his entry to Jerusalem, his last meal, his arrest, arraignment, and crucifixion. For us today these powerful events raise questions with ever greater urgency: Why was Jesus crucified? What difference did it make? Can this story still be meaningful for us? What new insights are waiting to spring forth from these texts?

The readings for Holy Week demand something more than brief homilies or meditations. Individuals might study the texts and this guide at home and then gather for Bible study each night. Holy Week might become an intense period for reflection—a retreat, a pilgrimage—that can bless not only the participants but the entire church.

It is crucial that this study guide be just that: not a substitute for the Bible but a guide through it. Read the scriptural text *before* tackling the commentary, so that the text is paramount in your interest and the commentary merely an aid to tease out thought. The guide has a particular point of view, but it is intended to be provocative, not prescriptive. It is a stimulus to thought, not a substitute for it. It can do its proper job only if you are working with an open Bible and entering into each text in turn. Then perhaps the Holy Spirit can use the words of this commentary to stir up the Word in you. That, at least, is my hope in writing this guide.

This study draws freely at points from my *Engaging the Powers: Discernment and Resistance in a World of Domination* (Fortress Press, 1992).

Sunday of the Passion
Palm Sunday

Lutheran	Roman Catholic	Episcopal	Common Lectionary
Zech. 9:9-10	Isa. 50:4-7	Isa. 45:21-25	Isa. 50:4-9a
Phil. 2:5-11	Phil. 2:6-11	Phil 2:5-11	Phil. 2:5-11
Mark 14:1—15:47	Mark 14:1—15:47	Mark 14:1—15:47 or Mark 15:1-39	Mark 14:1—15:47 or Mark 15:1-39

FIRST LESSON: ZECHARIAH 9:9-10

(Since Isa. 50:4-7 is used by all lectionaries on Wednesday of Holy Week, we will follow the Lutheran reading for Passion/Palm Sunday.)

The text of Zechariah is difficult to reconstruct. The English versions generally read, like the NRSV, "Lo, your king comes to you, triumphant and victorious is he." Both the Hebrew and the Greek (LXX), however, read "righteous and saving is he." Is the triumphalism of our versions influenced by the Christian picture of the "triumphal entry"? It is significant that both Matthew (21:5) and John (12:15) lack this reference to triumph when they cite Zech. 9:9-10. Perhaps our tradition has created victory when there was none. Unable to tolerate the "weakness" of God and the self-emptying of Christ (Phil. 2:5-11), have we created a victory parade when what took place on Palm Sunday was in fact more like a spoof, a lampooning, a burlesquing of normal views of kingly power?

It is quite possible that this satirization of domination is already present in the Zechariah text. Some scholars believe that 9:9-10 is a late interpolation into Zechariah which was already a composite of an earlier document from 520–518 B.C.E. (Zechariah 1–8), and a later, more apocalyptic piece written shortly after Alexander the Great's conquest of Palestine (chaps. 9–14). Although the materials are quite diverse and at times even outright contradictory (compare 9:10 with 9:13 and 10:3-5), their final form contains a clear brief for a new, nonviolent kingship. The Jews had learned, from the humiliations of captivity, a new kind of realism. Israel was too small to win its own battles. If God had further use for this people, God would have to protect them personally (2:4-5). "Not by might, nor by power, but by my spirit, says the Lord of hosts" (4:6) was to become the slogan, not just of Zechariah, but of a whole new approach to power that is just now beginning, in our own day, to bear fruit.

Exile had taught them something about the redeeming power of the small. Little Israel was to become the catalyst for the conversion of all the nations (2:11; 8:23; 9:7). Its Davidic king would forswear pomp and kingly might and bring benevolence and justice to light (3:8; 6:12; 7:9; 8:16; 12:8, 10, 12; 13:1). The Davidic family had become lowly and poor and disabused of the reliance on warfare that brought about the catastrophe of exile.

But, mysteriously (the text is extremely difficult), this king will have to suffer:

> And I will pour out a spirit of compassion and supplication on the house of David and the inhabitants of Jerusalem, so that, when they look on the one whom they have pierced, they shall mourn for him, as one mourns for an only child, and weep bitterly over him, as one weeps over a firstborn. (12:10)

They will "strike the shepherd, that the sheep may be scattered" (13:7). "And if anyone asks them, 'What are these wounds on your chest [Hebrew: wounds between your *hands*]?' the answer will be 'The wounds I received in the house of my friends' " (13:6).

So far as we know, this intimation was not developed into a suffering messiah expectation in early Judaism. They did not want to believe, any more than we do today, that God would bring deliverance through self-emptying and suffering.

SECOND LESSON: PHILIPPIANS 2:5-11

Zechariah had already stressed the humility of the new kind of king: "humble and riding on a donkey" (9:9). He would disarm, not the nations threatening Judah, but Judah itself: "He will cut off the chariot from Ephraim and the war horse from Jerusalem; and the battle bow shall be cut off, and he shall command peace to the nations." But he will achieve this peace by ruling over the entire then-known world (Zech. 9:10b).

Jesus presses these notions until they transform into an entirely new vision. He will not seek a kingdom for himself so that he can *impose* on the world the will of God. Although prophets and philosophers had anticipated parts of his program, no one, in the three thousand years since the rise of the conquest states in Mesopotamia, had formulated such a thoroughgoing repudiation of domination, nor has anyone since.

He challenged every assumption and tenet of the Domination System: The right of a few to exploit the many; the primacy of rich over poor, one race over others, men over women; the belief that the end justifies the use of any means, and that people can be used, even to their disadvantage, to get what one wants; that institutions, especially the state, are more important than people; and that God is the ultimate protector and guarantor of the absolute power of the state.

The values Jesus inculcated, and the vision he spread, were of an order free of domination of every kind: Where women and children enter the presence of God on a par with men; where nonviolence, love of enemies, and prayer for one's persecutors break the spiral of violence; where compassion, forgiveness, and acceptance of the marginalized create a new community free of class, racial, and gender distinctions. He abrogated purity regulations that separated insiders from outsiders, good from bad, and, ultimately, Jew from Gentile. He critiqued the law for having become captive to the very violence it was formulated to check, and for having become complicit in domination. He laid the foundation for the rejection of temple sacrifice and the belief that God requires sacral violence. God, he saw with a clarity unmatched since the exodus, was on the side not of the oppressive powers but of the oppressed. He called on his followers who wished to be first to become last, and to be, like him, a servant of all. He rejected titles, for himself or his disciples, and he transformed the master-student relationship by allowing women to study with him (Luke 10:38-42) and by calling his students "friends" (John 15:15).

He championed economic equality, and his band began to practice it. He blessed the poor, the meek, the mourners, as the very objects of God's deepest concern and the inheritors of the domination-free order. And that new order was already present wherever Jesus or his followers healed, exorcised demons, or proclaimed the good news.

But it was finally in the way he died that the radicality of everything he had taught was revealed. He died as he had lived. By taking his message to the center of the religious system, and to its colossal temple, with its tens of thousands of dependents and its massive economic generativity, Jesus challenged the darkness at the center of God's own holy people. Israel, too, had become enamored of the myth that violence redeems; that warfare and temple sacrifice are the means to national and spiritual safety; that domination is the name of the human game, and that if the Jews wanted to survive, they, too, would have to play it.

Israel, like the church after it, had become just like the other nations, hankering after the power to impose its will on the world. Domination had entered its life at every level. It projected onto the godhead endless violence, so much so that violence can be said to be the single most dominant theme of Scripture. But Israel differed from every other people in one respect: Violence had, for the first time, emerged as a problem for Israel. Israel had *not* engaged in violence in the exodus; God had done it for them. The prophets had already denounced blood sacrifice and military alliances; they objected to armed conflict in the present and prophesied a war-free world in the future.

In Jesus, God finally spoke this message through a life. Jesus not only said it, he lived it, he *was* it. Thus Paul's rhapsody in Philippians (quite possibly a hymn sung by the church) captures the paradox of Jesus' power: He did not consider violence as a means of becoming equal with God, as does Marduk in the Babylonian creation myth, but emptied himself, taking the form of a slave. He humbled himself—riding an ass, touching a leper, talking with children and women, washing his disciples' feet—and became obedient to the point of death, even death on a cross.

Paul's language is mythological, as if Jesus slid down a cloud into a human envelope and slid out again at his resurrection; but Paul is simply stating symbolically what really happened. Jesus really did live a life for others. He really did, literally, incarnate God in a human body. God was humanized, stripped of all the projections of violence. Jesus, we might even say, infiltrated the godhead (Luke 22:69). To call him Lord is simply to acknowledge that Jesus has now become the measure, not only of humanness, but of the divine. God, as it were, is now constrained by Jesus, defined by Jesus, revealed by Jesus. The lives of many others have revealed God. But who else has so transformed the way God is revealed, experienced, known? No wonder he has been given a name above every name.

GOSPEL: MARK 14:1—15:47

The lectionary for Year B ignores Jesus' entry into Jerusalem and instead takes in the full sweep of the passion narrative, which those who miss Holy Week observances would otherwise overlook entirely in moving straight from Palm Sunday to Easter Sunday. The purpose of an overview of such magnitude is to help us refocus on the meaning of the entire event: Why did the Powers That Be want Jesus killed? Why were they so desperate to get him out of the way?

When the Domination System catches the merest whiff of God's new order, by an automatic reflex it mobilizes all its might to suppress that order. Even before Jesus experienced its full fury against himself, he apparently predicted the outcome. The Powers are so immense, the opposition so weak, that every attempt at fundamental change seems doomed to failure. The Powers are seldom content merely to win; they must win big, in order to demoralize opposition before it can gain momentum. The tactics always include gratuitous violence, mocking derision, the intimidating brutality of the means of execution. All of this is standard, unexceptional. Jesus died just like all the others who challenged the powers that dominate the world.

Something went awry with Jesus, however. They scourged him with whips, but with each stroke of the lash their own illegitimacy was laid open. They mocked him with a robe and a crown of thorns, spitting on him and striking him on the head with a reed, ridiculing him with the ironic ovation "Hail, king of the Jews!"—not knowing that their acclamation would echo down the centuries. They stripped him naked and crucified him in humiliation, entirely unaware that this very act had stripped them of the last covering that disguised the towering wrongness of the whole way of living that their violence defended. They nailed him to the cross, not realizing that with each hammer's blow they were nailing up, for the whole world to see, the MENE, MENE, TEKEL, and PARSIN by which the Domination System would be numbered, weighed in the balances, found wanting, and finally terminated (Dan. 5:25-28).

What killed Jesus was not irreligion but religion itself; not lawlessness but precisely the law; not anarchy but the upholders of order. It was not the bestial but those considered best who crucified the one in whom the divine Wisdom was visibly incarnate. And because he was not only innocent, but the very embodiment of true religion, true law, and true order, this victim exposed their violence for what it was: not the defense of society but an attack against God.

How could this defeat issue in such a victory? The Powers were as powerful the day after the crucifixion as the day before. Nothing had visibly changed. And yet everything had changed.

For millennia the delusional system had taught that domination was a given in the nature of things. Now the cross revealed evil where one had always looked for good: in the guardians of the faith of the people, who safeguarded order by means of Roman violence.

The cross exposed as well humanity's complicity with the Powers, our willingness to trade away increments of freedom for installments of advantage. It shows us that we are now free to resist the claim of any finite thing as absolute or of any subsystem to be the whole.

The cross also exposes the Powers as unable to make Jesus become what they wanted him to be or to stop being who he was. Here was a person able to live out to the fullest what he felt was God's will. He chose to die rather than compromise with violence. The Powers threw at him every weapon in their arsenal, but they could not deflect him

11

from the trail that he and God were blazing. Because he lived thus, we too can walk that path.

Because they could not kill what was alive in him, the cross also revealed the impotence of death. Death is the Powers' final sanction. Jesus at his crucifixion neither fights the darkness nor flees under cover of it, but goes with it, goes into it. He enters the darkness, freely, voluntarily. The darkness is not dispelled or illuminated. It remains vast, untamed, void. But he somehow encompasses it. It becomes the darkness of God. It is now possible to enter any darkness and trust God to wrest from it meaning, coherence, resurrection.

Jesus' truth could not be killed. The massive forces arrayed in opposition to the truth are revealed to be puny over against the force of a free human being. The Chinese student who stood alone before a column of tanks for an eternity of minutes in Tiananmen Square graphically displayed this power. The collapse of Soviet and Eastern-bloc Communism is a breathtaking reminder that no evil can hold dominion indefinitely. As Martin Luther King, Jr., could see with a prophet's eyes, the universe bends toward justice.

Those who are freed from the fear of death are, as a consequence, able to break the spiral of violence. On the cross Jesus voluntarily took upon himself the violence of the entire system. "When he was abused, he did not return abuse; when he suffered, he did not threaten; but he entrusted himself to the one who judges justly" (1 Pet. 2:23). The cross is the ultimate paradigm of nonviolence. Through the cross God is revealing a new way, tried many times before, but now shown to be capable of consistent, programmatic embodiment.

Chai Ling was the Chinese student leader in Tiananmen Square when only five to ten thousand demonstrators were left, surrounded by the Red Army. She discovered that some students had machine guns. Calling them together, she told this story: A billion ants lived on a high mountain. A fire began at the base. It appeared that all billion of them would die. They made a ball and rolled down the mountain and through the fire to safety. But those on the surface died. We are the ones on the surface, she said; we must die for the people. So the students destroyed their weapons and sat down peacefully to wait for what seemed certain death. Perhaps as many as three thousand of them were killed. By refusing to use violence, they robbed the communist regime of its "mandate from heaven," guaranteeing its eventual collapse—or transformation.

Jesus' nonviolent response mirrored the very nature of God, who reaches out to a rebellious humanity through the cross in the only way that would not abridge our freedom. Had God not manifested divine

12

love toward us in an act of abject weakness, one that we experience as totally noncoercive and nonmanipulative (Phil. 2:5-11), the truth of our own being would have been forced on us rather than being something we freely choose. By this act of self-emptying, Jesus meets us, not at the apex of the pyramid of power, but at its base: "despised and rejected by others," a common criminal, the offscouring of all things.

As the Crucified, Jesus thus identifies with every victim of torture, incest, or rape; with every peasant caught in the cross fire of enemy patrols; with every single one of the forty thousand children who die each day of starvation. In his cry from the cross, "My God, my God, why have you forsaken me?" he is one with all doubters whose sense of justice overwhelms their capacity to believe in God; with every mother or father who cradles the lifeless body of a courageous son or daughter; with every Alzheimer's patient slowly losing the capacity of recognition. In Jesus we see the suffering of God with and in suffering people.

The cross is God's victory in another, unexpected way: In the act of exposing the Powers for what they are, Jesus nevertheless submitted to their authority as instituted by God. Jesus' way of nonviolence preserves respect for the rule of law even in the act of resisting oppressive laws. By submitting to the authority of the Powers, Jesus acknowledged their necessity but rejected the legitimacy of their pretentious claims. He submitted to their power to execute him, but in so doing relativized, deabsolutized, deidolized them, showing them to be themselves subordinate to the one who subordinated himself to them.

We, too, take up the cross of our tragic impotence and offer it to God, praying for light on the other side of the grave of hope. We want desperately for the world to have meaning, for things to work, for problems to have solutions. And if not? The cross also encompasses the meaninglessness, the sheer God-forsakenness we experience when we are crushed by the Powers.

Further, the cross is God's victory over the Powers because, in this event, the Christ-principle, which was incarnated and humanized in Jesus, was made universal, liberated to become the archetype of humanness for all who are drawn to him. Jesus fulfilled not only the Law and the Prophets of the Jews; he also fulfilled the myths of the pagans. He lived out not only the inner meaning of the old covenant, lifting it to a new plane. He also lived out, in the daily pattern of his life and teaching and in an exemplary way in his death and resurrection, the pattern of dying and rising known to myths around the globe. What these myths depicted as the necessary course of personal and social development, Jesus demonstrated as an actual human possibility.

In so doing, his own history became mythic, universal. By historicizing these myths he mythicized his history. At the same time, he demystified these myths by exposing the actual sociopolitical agents of this dying. The timeless pattern of dying and rising is thus historicized as the struggle to humanize existence in the face of Powers that employ death as their final sanction.

Jesus' death on the cross was like a black hole in space that sucked into its collapsing vortex the very meaning of the universe, until in the intensity of its compaction there was an explosive reversal, and the stuff of which galaxies are made was blown out into the universe. So Jesus as the cosmic Christ became universal, the truly Human One, and as such, the bearer of our own utmost possibilities for living.

Killing Jesus was like trying to destroy a dandelion seed-head by blowing on it. It was like shattering a sun into a million fragments of light.

Monday in Holy Week

Lutheran	Roman Catholic	Episcopal	Common Lectionary
Isa. 42:1-9	Isa. 42:1-7	Isa. 42:1-9	Isa. 42:1-9
Heb. 9:11-15		Heb. 11:39—12:3	Heb. 9:11-15
John 12:1-11	John 12:1-11	John 12:1-11 *or* Mark 14:3-9	John 12:1-11

FIRST LESSON: ISAIAH 42:1-9

This is the first song of the Servant of the Lord (*ebed Yahweh*). Who is this servant? The Hebrew text regards this figure as an individual, ordained by God to carry out a redemptive task. The Greek version of the Hebrew Bible, however, reads it as collective: "*Jacob* my servant, whom I uphold, *Israel* my chosen one, whom my soul awaits/welcomes." The New Testament reads it, once again, as individual and regards it as Jesus. The church later reads it as collective and applies it to us.

That is, the task allotted to the servant figure is at once personal and collective. It points to the *ebed Yahweh*, the servant of the Lord, and it points to Jesus. But it also points to Israel and to the church. For the task is monumental, overwhelming, and beyond human capability. Only God can do it, and God can do it only through us.

Can we hear this freshly? We have here one of the most universalized visions ever proclaimed. The servants of the Lord are assigned to bring justice not simply to Israel but to all the nations. This impossible task will be possible because God's spirit will be upon them (v. 1). Gone are the dreams of a despotism of the good, a benevolent tyrant who will impose on all the justice God desires. This servant does not cry out nor resort to street preaching. God's chosen is gentle, compassionate, patient, and there is no question that success will attend the effort.

All very optimistic. But we remember that this is Monday of Holy Week, and the victory still eludes our grasp. Yet God places the imprimatur of the creation itself on the promise:

> Thus says God, the Lord,
>> who created the heavens and stretched them out,
>> who spread out the earth and what comes from it,
> who gives breath to the people upon it
>> and spirit to those who walk in it:
> I am the Lord, I have called you in righteousness. (vv. 5-6a)

If God created from nothing the things that are, and the entire universe from a dot of energy no larger than the period that ends a sentence (and where did the dot come from?), can the same God not find a way to establish justice among fratricidal humans?

Israel is chosen, it is true, but not for its own sake or advantage: "I have given you as a covenant to the people, a light to the nations" (v. 6). Its task is unique: to provide a critique of domination. It alone is able to testify to the universality of God, to free idolaters from the delusions that fixate them on a mere aspect of that mysterious creation (v. 8). Israel alone can open the eyes blinded by greed and power and bring out of prison those who are captive to dreams of conquest, violence, and oppression. In short, Israel is special, not because of any spiritual genius it possesses or because it alone practices righteousness (it did not and it does not), but because, by virtue of the astonishing grace of the exodus, Israel has seen what no other people has known: that God is on the side of the oppressed, the victim, the little people. Every other people understood the divine to be the legitimizer of kings and priesthoods; Israel alone was given to see that God opposes kings and priesthoods and is growing a new order from below, like seed sprouting up toward the kingdom of God.

This is a new thing. It is still new, still unheard, still disdained. What Israel once proclaimed alone the church now shares. In the face of monolithic opposition, church and synagogue must unite for their single task: to call humanity away from the brink of self-destructive violence; to establish justice for all; to inculcate the values of God against the values of conquest, militarism, consumerism, ethnic hostilities, economic inequities, and greed. The new thing God does in Jesus is still the old thing God was doing through Israel all along: trying to win followers for the new world coming.

SECOND LESSON: HEBREWS 9:11-15

That new world is ushered in by sacrificial blood. But therein lies a host of difficulties. Why is sacrifice necessary? How did blood sacrifice get started in the first place? Does God really need it? The Epistle to the Hebrews attempted to answer those questions, and in doing so, created one great new question: Is Christ's sacrifice the abrogation and *end* of sacrificing, or is it the *final* sacrifice? That is, did Jesus' death on the cross unmask the horror at the heart of religion, with its endless slaughter of animals to appease the wrath of God, or was it the ultimate sacrifice, one so perfect as to require no further sacrificing ever? Does the crucifixion, the rending of the temple veil, the discernment that the new community was the temple of the Holy Spirit, complete the prophetic repudiation of sacrifice (Isa. 1:11-17; 17:7-8; 66:3; Jer. 6:20; 7:21-23, 31; 14:12; Hos. 6:6; 9:4; Amos 5:21-27; Micah 6:6-8; see also Pss. 40:6; 50:13-14; 51:16-17), or does it accept all the premises of the sacrificial cultus and merely assert that Jesus has satisfied these criteria in so exemplary a way that no additional sacrifice is conceivable?

The difference is crucial, for in that distinction lies a whole world of theological difference. The gospel denounces the execution of Jesus as a total miscarriage of justice, a perfect example of untruth, a crime against God. The Gospels are at pains to show that the charges against Jesus do not hold water, not in order to avoid suspicion of subversion but precisely to reveal the scapegoating mechanism. The enemy of the state and of religion is, in fact, an innocent victim. His arraignment, trial, crucifixion, and death reveal, at last, for all the world to see, the scapegoating mechanism that has existed at the heart of religion and has justified sacral violence. God is revealed, not as demanding sacrifice, but as taking the part of the sacrificed.

The earliest Christians were not able to sustain the intensity of this revelation and dimmed it by confusing God's intention to *reveal* the scapegoating mechanism for what it was with the notion that God *intended* Jesus' death. This in turn led to their reinserting the new revelation into the scapegoat theology: Jesus was sent by God to be the *last* scapegoat and to reconcile us, once and for all, to God. Which view undergirds the Epistle to the Hebrews?

The earliest epistles and all the Gospels had attested that Jesus was executed by the Powers. Jesus' own view of his inevitable death at the hands of the Powers seems to have been that God's nonviolent reign could come only in the teeth of desperate opposition and the violent recoil of the Domination System. In time, however, Christian theology came to argue that *God* was the one who provided Jesus as a lamb sacrificed in our stead; that God was the angry and aggrieved party who must be placated by blood sacrifice; that God was, finally, both sacrificer and sacrificed. Jesus therefore ceased to be a man executed for his integrity and became a "Godman who can offer to God adequate expiation for us all" (Basil).

Rather than God triumphing over the Powers through Jesus' non-violent self-sacrifice on the cross, the Powers disappeared from discussion, and God was involved in a transaction wholly within God's own self. But what is wrong with this God, that the legal ledgers can be balanced only by means of the death of an innocent victim? Jesus simply declared people forgiven, confident that he spoke the mind of God. Why then is a sacrificial victim necessary to make forgiveness possible? Does not the death of Jesus reveal that all such sacrifices are unnecessary?

The God whom Jesus revealed as no longer our rival, no longer threatening and vengeful, but unconditionally loving and forgiving, who needed no satisfaction by blood—this God of infinite mercy was metamorphosed by the church into the image of a wrathful God whose demand for blood atonement led God to require the death of his own Son on behalf of us all. The nonviolent God of Jesus came to be depicted as a God of unequaled violence, since God not only allegedly demanded the blood of the victim who was closest and most precious to him, but also held the whole of humanity accountable for a death that God both anticipated and required. Against such an image of God the revolt of atheism is an act of pure religion.

The God whom Jesus reveals, by contrast, refrains from all forms of reprisal and demands no victims. Jesus "himself bore our sins in his body on the cross" (1 Pet. 2:24), not to reconcile God to us, as the blood atonement theory has it, but to reconcile us to God (2 Cor. 5:18). God has renounced any accounting of sins; no repayment is required or even possible. God is not a stern and inflexible magistrate but a loving Abba.

Why then was a redemptive act necessary? Because our resentment toward God and our will to kill leave us unable to turn to God. God does not need to be appeased, but rather we need to be delivered from our hatred and rebellion against God. God, therefore, takes the initiative, providing proof, by Jesus' own self-offering, of God's infinitely forgiving love.

Only by being driven out by violence could God signal to humanity that the divine is nonviolent and is antithetical to the kingdom of violence. As Simone Weil put it, the false God changes suffering into violence, the true God changes violence into suffering. Jesus' message reveals that those who believe in divine violence are still mired in Satan's universe. To be this God's offspring requires the unconditional and unilateral renunciation of violence. The reign of God means the complete and definitive elimination of every form of violence between individuals and nations.

According to the Christus Victor, or social theory, of the atonement, what Christ has overcome is not God's "wrath" but precisely the Powers themselves. The forgiveness of which the gospel speaks is forgiveness for complicity in our own oppression and in that of others. Our alienation is not solely the result of our rebellion against God. It is also the way we have been socialized by alienating rules and requirements. We do not freely surrender our authenticity; it is stolen from us by the Powers. Before we reach the age of choice, our choices have already been to a high degree chosen for us by a system indifferent to our uniqueness. Therefore Jesus "gave himself for our sins to set us free from this Domination Epoch" (*aion*—Gal. 1:4*).

In its early centuries, the church lived in nonviolent conflict with the Roman Empire and used the imagery of conflict to explain the efficacy of the cross. God and Satan were engaged in cosmic struggle. Two irreconcilable systems strove for the allegiance of humanity. The Christus Victor, or social theory, of the atonement proclaimed release of the captives to those who had formerly been deluded and enslaved by the Domination System, and it set itself against that system with all its might.

With the conversion of Constantine, however, the Empire assumed from the church the role of God's providential agent in history. Once Christianity became the religion of the Empire, its success was linked to the success of the Empire, and *preservation of the Empire became the decisive criterion for ethical behavior.* The Christus Victor theology fell out of favor, not because of intrinsic inadequacies, but because it was subversive to the church's role as state religion. The church saw the demonic as lodged no longer in the Empire but in the Empire's enemies. Atonement became a highly individual transaction between the believer and God; society was assumed to be Christian, so the idea that the work of Christ entails the radical critique of society was largely abandoned.

Christianity has, on the whole, succeeded no more than Judaism in unmasking the violence at the core of humanity's religions. Its accommodation to power politics through the infinitely malleable ideology of the just war, its abandonment of the Christus Victor, or social theory, of the atonement for the blood theory, its projection of the reign of God into an afterlife or the remote future—all this gutted the church's message of its most radical elements. The mass (in the theology of the Council of Trent) became a perpetual sacrifice rather than the end of all need for sacrifice; and all Jews were scapegoated for the death of Jesus, so that the cycle of slaughter was set loose to run its violent course all over again.

Nevertheless, the story was there for all to read in the Gospels, and it continues to work, like a time-release capsule, liberating those crushed by a legalistic, wrathful pseudo-Christianity from false images of God and murderous false guilt.

GOSPEL: JOHN 12:1-11

The anointing story that appears in all four Gospels seems to be a composite of two separate accounts. One is set in Galilee, in the home of a Pharisee, where a penitent sinner enters and weeps in Jesus' presence. Her tears fall on his feet, and she wipes them with her hair, kissing his feet. The anointing may be lacking here altogether. The other is set in Bethany in the home of Simon the leper, where a woman anoints Jesus' feet with costly perfume as an expression of love (Raymond E. Brown, *The Gospel according to John,* The Anchor Bible [Garden City, N.Y.: Doubleday, 1966], 450). John's account combines elements of both. As a consequence, it is difficult to know what the real point of the story is. In Luke it is forgiveness; in Matthew and Mark, remembrance of her act of anointing him before his death. But John's version has been reworked beyond intelligibility. Why does Mary anoint his feet rather than his head? Perhaps the fourth evangelist changed an original reference to her anointing his head (as in Matthew and Mark) to feet in order to downplay any hint of messianic anointing; Jesus for this evangelist is far more than mere messiah; he is Son of God (Robert T. Fortna, *The Fourth Gospel and Its Predecessor* [Philadelphia: Fortress, 1988], 142). But her wiping of his feet with her hair is thereby rendered absurd: Why wipe off what she had so graciously put on?

The intrusion of the motif of Judas's greed further compounds confusion. Here he is tarred as a thief who complains about the waste of the nard, not out of concern for the poor but because he wants to get his hands on the proceeds of its sale. This defamation of Judas's character is unworthy of the Gospel and must be seen for what it is: an unforgiving hostility that has not yet been purified by the filter of the cross.

Jesus' response to Mary's act in John is also puzzling; she is to keep the remainder of the ointment for the day of his burial. But that motif is never alluded to again. On the day of his death, instead, Nicodemus, "who had at first come to Jesus by night, also came, bringing a mixture of myrrh and aloes, weighing about a hundred pounds," with which to anoint him for burial (John 19:39). So what then is the point of Jesus' saying in 12:7?

In 12:9-11, however, we hear the ungarbled voice of the evangelist. The resurrection of Lazarus, Jesus' greatest sign, was having its effect on the "great crowd of the Jews," who were now flocking to see, not just Jesus, but the dead man made alive. Rather than enhancing Jesus' success, however, it provoked the authorities to add Lazarus to their hit list, "since it was on account of him that many of the Jews were deserting and were believing in Jesus." But then we hear nothing more of this projected execution of Lazarus.

In short, this might be a good time to dust off the Epistle to the Hebrews.

Tuesday in Holy Week

Lutheran	Roman Catholic	Episcopal	Common Lectionary
Isa. 49:1-6	Isa. 49:1-6	Isa. 49:1-6	Isa. 49:1-7
1 Cor. 1:18-25		1 Cor. 1:18-31	1 Cor. 1:18-31
John 12:20-36	John 13:21-33, 36-38	John 12:37-38, 42-50 or Mark 11:15-19	John 12:20-36

FIRST LESSON: ISAIAH 49:1-6

This is the second song of the Servant of the Lord. In the years of Babylonian exile, such fantastic visions as Second Isaiah indulged in must have seemed quixotic to Jewish hearers. Not only would Israel be redeemed from captivity, but it would become a light to all the nations. Tiny Israel: Such dreams must have struck the sober minded as megalomania. If God wished to reach the ends of the earth with the knowledge of God, God should have chosen a nation capable of subduing peoples to the ends of the earth. Surely it is to the great conquest nations—Assyria, Babylon, Alexander the Great and his successors, Rome—that one must look if one wants to propagate a message to the world, not to one of its smallest tribes!

No wonder the prophet feels overwhelmed, as one who has labored in vain. Such promises are too grandiose; who will believe them? In such moments of doubt the prophet reaffirms the original call of God. The prophetic vocation is all that he can cling to. And that vocation was ordained, not in a recent moment of time, but from his mother's womb. From birth everything that had gone into shaping the prophet conspired to make his tongue like a sharp sword or a polished arrow. And from birth God had protected the prophet from the hatred and envy of those who recognized unfailingly that the prophet spoke a truth from God. They knew it was from God, and knew they knew it, and yet they refused to listen and stopped their ears and, if necessary, would stop the prophet's mouth. Yet, despite opposition, the prophet declares, God has carried him in the shadow of his hand and hidden him in his quiver. The prophet is expendable for God, and God in turn honors the prophet.

Once more, in this second Servant Song, ambiguity prevails as to the servant's identity. Is it one person, or all Israel? Once again the answer seems to be, both. "And God said to me": surely the prophet is addressed; yet the message is "You are my servant, *Israel,* in whom I will be glorified." Insofar as the prophet embraces Israel's own vocation, the prophet is Israel. Just so, at his baptism Jesus embodies *Israel's* vocation, taking on the role of the *ebed* (servant/son) of Yahweh ("You are my *ebed,* the Beloved, with you I am well pleased"—Mark 1:11// Isa. 42:1). Likewise, Jesus in the wilderness recapitulates Israel's temptations in the wilderness, succeeding where they failed. The church, too, assumes the role of Israel insofar it becomes a light to the nations. The gospel, one might say, is simply Judaism universalized, made accessible to all humanity.

The church today, demoralized with declining memberships and the graying of its congregations, is no more ready to hear God reiterate these promises than was Israel in exile. Faced with the constant threat of assimilation and declining interest in the holy land as new generations came along who had never seen it, Israel was in imminent danger of abandoning its vocation in the name of sheer survival—just like churches today. To such as we the Word of the Lord comes, just as it did to and through Second Isaiah: It is too light a thing that you should be my servants to raise up the church of Christ; I will give you as a light to the nations, that my salvation may reach to the end of the earth.

God's word will not return empty. It will accomplish what is promised. So strengthen the weak knees, and listen for the far-off triumph song, for God will surely do it. The Word of the Lord. Thanks be to God!

SECOND LESSON: 1 CORINTHIANS 1:18-31

Two Greek words are key to deciphering this passage: "world" and "age." The first, "world" (*kosmos*), can mean the creation, the universe, humanity, the planet Earth, the theater of history. But in this passage, and frequently in the Gospel of John, "world" refers to *the human sociological realm that exists in estrangement from God.* The special New Testament sense of world as an alienating and alienated ethos may be translated more meaningfully as "system."

In South Africa, for example, many blacks are fully aware that they are fighting the apartheid system, not merely white people. They know that they cannot gain freedom simply by changing the color of the people at the top and leaving the system intact. When police are at the door, people inside will warn, "The System is here." When they see propaganda on television, they quip, "The System is lying again." Of a strike: "We're struggling against the System." The most effective

way to get a black to stop behaving in collusion with the government, Albert Nolan comments, is to say, "You are supporting the System."

Thus, when Paul writes, "Has not God made foolish the wisdom of the world?" he is indicting not the created order but the humanly contrived "knowledge" of reality that has excluded the living God from its center. Whenever Christians have understood Paul's caustic remarks about the folly of this world as meaning that the *physical world* is evil, they have tended to reject the created order, sexuality, and even their own bodies, and to manifest open contempt for efforts at political change. "System" yields an entirely different meaning, however, one far closer to Paul's intent, which cannot have been to despise the creation that he himself affirms was created by God. But the Domination System *does* reject God and tries to fashion a pseudoreality that legitimates oppression, exploitation, greed, violence, patriarchy, hierarchicalism, classism, racism, and other forms of domination. Rejection of the *kosmos,* as John H. Elliott remarks, is not antiworldly but antiestablishment.

The other key term is "age" (*aion*). Just as the imagery of *kosmos* is spacial or systemic, that of *aion* is temporal. It conjures up a vision, not of the structure of reality, but of the flow of time from its inception: "time like an ever-flowing stream." Hence it could be used for the created order in its temporal ongoingness: God "created the *aions*" or world-periods (Heb. 1:2). The present world-period, however, is under the power of evil. Here again, as with *kosmos,* the term *aion* takes on a negative sense in some New Testament passages. Thus the *kosmos* can be called "the present evil epoch [*aion*]" (Gal. 1:4*), organized under Satan, "the god of this world-period [*aion*]" who "has blinded the minds of the unbelievers, to keep them from seeing the light of the gospel of the glory of Christ" (2 Cor. 4:4*). Even Satan's subordinates can be characterized by their relationship to this period: They are "the *archons* [rulers] of this *aion,* who are doomed to perish" (1 Cor. 2:6*; see also 2:8).

This period is not just fallen time, time characterized by the loss of presence, clock time, time ticking down toward death, time as a commodity not to be wasted, an enemy that must be "fought," a precious fluid that we cannot hold in our hands. All these point to natural human finitude. But time under the sway of the Domination System becomes more sinister. It marks the intolerable extension of oppression from generation to generation and century to century, presided over by Satan, the god of the Domination Epoch.

Liberation thus must involve the healing of our relationship to time. We must "redeem the time," as Col. 4:5 (KJV) puts it. Evil in history was not always present; it had an origin in time. Likewise, evil will not always exist; it has an end in time, when "this *aion*" is superseded by "the *aion* to come" (Matt. 12:32*). Like the world, time is good, fallen, and must itself be redeemed.

If we understand "world" as the Domination System, and *aion* as the Domination Epoch, we can paraphrase the passage thus:

> Where is the intellectual? Where is the scholar? Where is the debater whose premises are all taken from this Domination Epoch [*aion*]? Has not God rendered ridiculous the wisdom of the Domination System [*kosmos*]? For since, in the craftiness of God, the Domination System [*kosmos*] did not know God through wisdom, God decided, through the nonsense that we declare, to save those who believe. . . . Consider your own call, brothers and sisters; not many of you were wise as the Domination System counts wisdom [*kata sarka*]; not many were powerful, not many were of noble birth. But God chose what is foolish to the Domination System [*kosmos*] to shame the wise; God chose what is weak in the eyes of the Domination System [*kosmos*] to shame the strong; God chose what is low and despised by the Domination System [*kosmos*], things that are mere nothings, to reduce to nothing things that are, so that no one might boast in the presence of God.

The New Testament is unequivocal: Those who have sold their souls to domination cannot comprehend the new reality of Jesus. Pilate, as Rome's representative, does not and cannot understand that another order of reality is breaking in on the hegemony of violence that, under the temporary guise of Rome, now straddles the world. Jesus answers him: "The New Reality [*basileia*] of which I speak is not of this old System of Domination [*kosmos*]; if it were, my aides would fight, that I not be delivered to the Jewish authorities. But the New Reality of which I speak does not take its rise from the Domination System [*kosmos*]" (John 18:36). How different that sounds from the usual translation, "My kingdom is not of this world"! The values of the Domination System and those of Jesus are incommensurable. Violence cannot cure violence. The New Reality eschews violence, but it has its own, quite amazing forms of power, which those inured to violence cannot comprehend.

So also the Epistle of James: "Has not God chosen those who are poor in the Domination System to be rich in faith and heirs of the New Reality [*basileia*] that he has promised to those who love God?" (2:5*). "Do you not know that friendship with the Domination System is enmity with God?" (James 4:4*).

Those who once had no hope and were without God in the System (*kosmos*) (Eph. 2:12), who have now had their eyes opened, must jettison the socialization that held them complicit in their own oppression and that of others.

Do not love the Domination System [*kosmos*] or the things pertaining to it. If anyone loves that System [*kosmos*], the love of the Abba is not in that person. For everything in that System [*kosmos*]—the desire engendered by an alienated body and a wandering eye and the arrogant pretensions of those who are full of themselves—is not of Abba but is begotten by the Domination System itself. That System is passing away with all its perverse desires, but the person who does what God wants done remains into the epoch [*aion*] that is coming. (1 John 2:15-17*)

Those liberated from the tyranny of the old order receive a new, holy spirit—"not the spirit of the Domination System [*kosmos*],"—that would be Satan—"but the Spirit that is from God" (1 Cor. 2:12*); "the Spirit of truth, which the Domination System is not able to receive, because it can neither recognize it nor comprehend it. You know it, because it is already in your midst, and will be inside your very being" (John 14:17*). This new Spirit resocializes believers into the New Reality.

Not only do those liberated from the old System receive a new Spirit, they receive a new world. "What is real," asserts Jürgen Habermas, "is that which can be experienced according to the interpretations of a prevailing symbolic system." Most symbolic systems have served to shore up the power and privileges of those at the top. In the New Testament, by contrast, the insights of the exodus were expanded by the revelation of the cross and resurrection; the particularity of a slave revolt by an oppressed people, the Israelites, was universalized by the recognition of the nature of the Domination System. Consequently, those whose eyes had been opened by the exodus and the cross now saw a different reality, a new "world." What had been invisible—the all-pervasive exploitation of the many by the few—was rendered visible, judged, and found wanting. Those with this new sight needed no longer to subject themselves to the delusions that formerly shaped their alienated picture of "world."

In that Spirit, Paul can exult, "May I never boast of anything except the cross of our Lord Jesus Christ, by which the Domination System [*kosmos*]"—which crucified Jesus—"has been crucified to me, and I to that System" (Gal. 6:14*). The Johannine community also celebrates the great reversal of the cross: "In the old System you face persecution. But take courage," Jesus says, "I have vanquished the Domination System!" (John 16:33*). The disciples are still "in" the System (John 17:11), but not of it: "If the System hates you, be aware that it hated me before it hated you. If you would collaborate with the System, the System would love you for it; but because you have turned your backs on it (because I have extricated you from the System!), it hates you" (John 15:18-19*). "Do not be astonished, brothers and sisters, that the System hates you" (1 John 3:13*). "For whatever is born of God conquers the Domination System. And this is the victory that overcomes that System: our faith" (1 John 5:4*).

However it comes, then, God's system will replace the Domination System, not by violent confrontation, but as increasing numbers of people find themselves drawn toward its values: "You see, you can do nothing. Look, the *kosmos* has gone after him" (John 12:19). Only God can bring about a new system in its entirety; a new kind of earthly existence will be given us by the selective process itself. And yet, though it cannot be built, it is our task to try to create the conditions that would make that selection possible. Prayer, persuasion, and social struggle thus occupy the community that lives "as if" God's reign has already begun.

Until the new order of God arrives, believers are "to deal with the old System as though they had no dealings with it. For the basic structure [*schema*] of the dominant System [*kosmos*] is passing away" (1 Cor. 7:31*). "I do not pray that you should take them out of the System," for that is the theater in which God's sovereignty must be established, "but that you keep them from the evil one," that is, from succumbing to its spirituality (John 17:15*). The Domination System will attempt to crush every vestige of authentic living. "The System has hated them, because they have disavowed allegiance to the System" (John 17:14*). "If you belonged to the System, the System would love you as its own. Because you do not belong to the System, but I have chosen you out of the System—therefore the System hates you" (John 15:19*). Ignatius of Antioch, martyred for his faith in about the year 107, perceptively observed that "the greatness of Christianity lies in its being hated by the world [read Domination System], not in its being convincing to it." "You will weep and mourn," says John, "but the System will rejoice;" like a woman in travail, "you will have pain, but your pain will turn into joy" (John 16:20), as you help midwife the birth of a new and happier system.

GOSPEL: JOHN 12:20-36

The lesson in John's Gospel continues the sharp distinction between Jesus' message and the brainwashing perpetrated on us by "this world." "Those who hate their life in this System [*kosmos*] will keep it for *aionic* life" (12:25*). This is not an injunction to self-loathing but a very down-to-earth observation: Only those who find their lives detestable under the Powers That Be will have the courage to reject the latter's overblown authority. "Now is the judgment of the Domination System; now the ruler of this System will be driven out" (v. 31*). But it will be Jesus himself who is driven out, the scapegoat who ends all scape-goating. The Domination System is not defeated by domination means. God has a screwy wisdom that we have not yet taken the measure of.

Paul had said, in our second lesson, that the gospel was foolishness to Greeks. According to John, some Greeks wish to see Jesus, and Jesus delivers to them the tightest set of mind-snapping paradoxes in the Gospel. The Human Being ("son of man") will be glorified—by being crucified. Wheat lives—by dying. Those who love their lives in an alienated and alienating system will lose them, and those who hate them in our world as presently constituted will keep them. Then he issues an elliptical call to discipleship (v. 26) that has no recorded result; these Greeks vanish into thin air. Greeks desire wisdom; they must have thought it foolishness.

Yes, and Jews seek signs, just as Paul had said. If only the heavens would open and the divine voice endorse him! Then we would believe. So God and Jesus put on a little show, and the crowd nullifies it in a debate over whether it was thunder or an angel. Nothing comes of either his wisdom or his signs. Jesus is not surprised. Still exactly paralleling Paul, the evangelist eschews wisdom and signs and focuses solely on the cross. All the voice from heaven does is repeat what Jesus had said five verses before (v. 23): He will be glorified through death. It will be the cross that lifts him up and exalts him, not kingly power. It will be through the executioner's gibbet that he will draw all people to himself, not through a clever ad campaign. This cross will judge the world, because it will reveal the scapegoating mechanism for what it is. This cross will drive out the "ruler of the Domination System," Satan, because it exposes the impotence of state force and religious dogma to silence truth. It will dispel the darkness of the present world order the way a single candle conquers the blackest night.

But the light is not just the message, the truth, the judgment. It is a person. The Human Being, Jesus, *is* light. In him we see humanness incarnate, accomplished, actualized. We see what we are destined to become. "Beloved, we are God's children now; what we will be has not yet been revealed. What we do know is this: when he is revealed, we will be like him, for we will see him as he is" (1 John 3:2). We, too, are to become light, incarnate light. So "believe in the light, so that you may become children of light" (John 12:36).

Thus speaking the last words of his public ministry in John's Gospel, Jesus goes into hiding. There are those who hate the light and seek to snuff out every candle.

Wednesday in Holy Week

Lutheran	Roman Catholic	Episcopal	Common Lectionary
Isa. 50:4-9a	Isa. 50:4-9a	Isa. 50:4-9a	Isa. 50:4-9a
Rom. 5:6-11		Heb. 9:11-15, 24-28	Heb. 12:1-3
Matt. 26:14-25	Matt. 26:14-25	John 13:31-35 *or* Matt. 26:1-5, 14-25	John 13:21-30

FIRST LESSON: ISAIAH 50:4-9a

This is the third song of the Servant of the Lord. The *ebed Yahweh* is the perfect image of receptivity and openness, able to sustain the weary with a word because God wakens the servant's ear to listen as those who are taught. Nor was the servant of the Lord rebellious or cowardly; when those who heard the prophetic rebuke beat the servant's back or plucked out his beard or spat in his face and heaped the prophet with insults, God set the servant's face like flint. One with God is a majority. God will vindicate the prophetic word with fact, events, truth, reality. The prophet is content.

This may strike some of us as superhuman fidelity. We often do *not* know how to sustain the weary with a word. Instead we are acutely in need of sustenance ourselves. Who is more weary than we? The servants of the Lord nowadays are more likely to exhibit symptoms of burnout than to be sustainers.

Perhaps the key is listening. It is hard for us to believe that time spent listening is not precious time wasted. But if we are to have the tongue of one who is taught and an ear to listen as one who is spoken to, then we will need to prioritize our time according to a different set of values. Our reluctance is not due to our being so frightfully busy; we still take time to eat and sleep and make love. It is because so many of us are functional atheists. We simply do not believe that God will speak to us. If we did, how could we *not* take the time?

SECOND LESSON: ROMANS 5:6-11

Nowhere does Paul rise to greater heights of clarity about the redemptive act of God in Christ than here. On the one hand is humanity—weak, without the strength to save itself, unable to ascend to God. On the other is God, yearning for reconciliation with a rebellious humanity. Since we could not extricate ourselves from the strands of the web in which we were caught, God took the full initiative by sending Jesus, who hurled himself into the center of the web, snapping all its strands and setting the captives free.

It is an eternal affront to humanity that it cannot save itself. Our infantile omnipotence, out of which we never seem to grow, seethes with fury at being unable to be omnicompetent as well. To be utterly helpless to achieve the fullness of our lives, our selves, our societies, rankles us to the core. Surely better education, better families, better churches, better politicians can cure our ills! Consequently, God's self-offering does not please us in the least. A God like this is an insult to our capacities. Such a God must be disposed of as quickly as possible. Jesus is not even allowed to detail his five-year plan. His life is snuffed out almost as soon as he begins.

Why? A life brimming so full of God, of vitality, of truth, is not just a lure but an accusation. Beside such a yardstick, our lives are tawdry, empty, minuscule, pathetic, and wrong. Rather than greet so great a revelation with joy, we receive it as a reproach. God is, once again, condemning us—not, this time, by threatening to judge us but by dangling before us so overwhelming a possibility of transformation. Such change will be too painful. And it will require letting go of the littleness that we are in order to grasp the greatness we are offered.

So humanity destroys the revealer, only to be blasted by a light blinding in its brilliance: Having tried to kill the God we saw in Jesus, we now see a God who loves us despite our attempted deicide. What kind of God is this, who offers God's own being as proof of love? What greater love is conceivable? Conceivable?—such an idea could never have been conceived by the human brain. It could only have been shown us. The idea itself is unthinkable. If God wants relationship with us so desperately, yearns for us, longs for us, dies for us, even when we turn on such grace with murderous hate, then nothing we can do or could ever do will make such a God stop loving us. And if that is true, then our near-certainty that we are unlovable is proven false.

What an astonishing God!

In all this, Paul only once hints that God's wrath must be appeased (5:9). But that text only says, "We will be saved through him from the wrath" (NRSV adds "of God"). Its source is not specified. In Rom. 1:18-32, Paul has already specified what that wrath is: God's giving us up to the consequences of our own actions. The wrath is having to accept responsibility for the wrong we have done. Wrath is being forced to drink the water we pollute and breathe the air we poison. Wrath is having to bury the children murdered on our school yards by the people who buy the machine guns we refuse to outlaw. Wrath is having to negotiate treacherous streets in fear of attack by an underclass that we have permanently dispossessed. Wrath is teaching people that they are of no intrinsic, divine value, and then dealing with their inability to feel remorse when they blow other people away with their weapons.

This vicious circle of acts and consequences has been broken by the death of Jesus. Now the wrath is no longer a brute fate but a challenge to change. The unbelievable demonstration of God's seeking love finds us in our webs and pulls us out. We are empowered to become more of who God made us to be. We see in Jesus the possibilities of our own fuller lives, and the long-dormant potential laid up in us through our creation is aroused. We want to become. We become alive. We find ourselves gradually being stripped of all that is inauthentic. We are cleansed and forgiven for all the ways we have violated our own and others' lives. We are slowly extricated from the Domination System. We begin to discover the divine ecology. And all this comes from God, at God's gracious initiative.

GOSPEL: MATTHEW 26:14-25; JOHN 13:21-30

How are the three texts for Wednesday of Holy Week related? I have no idea. Whoever put them together must know something I have totally missed. But no matter; the lectionary is scarcely canonical. The three texts can also stand very well alone. So, to the Gospel.

Why did Judas betray Jesus? Four theories deserve mention: (1) Judas was greedy and did it for money; (2) Judas was a zealot who became disillusioned with Jesus when he failed to precipitate armed revolt; and (3) Satan entered into Judas and caused the betrayal.

1. John's Gospel portrays Judas as incensed at the waste of the ointment that Mary poured on Jesus' feet. " 'Why was this perfume not sold for three hundred denarii and the money given to the poor?' (He said this not because he cared about the poor, but because he was a thief; he kept the common purse and used to steal what was put into it)" (John 12:5-6). Matthew and Mark preserve the same order of stories (the anointing followed by Judas's betrayal), but they ascribe the outrage to the disciples or "others" generally. Had Matthew and Luke been in possession of a tradition that helped explain Judas's defection, they would surely have used it. Consequently it would appear that John has invented this detail. There is something sub-Christian in this account; the mystery of iniquity is papered over by an attack on Judas's character that makes incomprehensible Jesus' choise of him as a disciple.

Not only that, John also apparently deploys Judas on Jesus' left at the banquet, which would certainly be a place of honor (Raymond E.

Brown, *The Gospel according to John*, 2:574). If Judas was just a rotten apple, why did Jesus not exclude him from the fellowship far earlier? If Judas had just been greedy, why would he have accepted such a ridiculous pittance for a payment (thirty pieces of silver equalled damages for the life of a slave gored by an ox [Exod. 21:32], but in the first century worth only a tenth of that) or (as Matthew has it) attempted to return the tainted money (27:3-5)?

2. Another popular theory about Judas is built around his nickname "Iscariot," which may refer to his membership in the Sicarii, a conspiracy of fanatical nationalists dedicated to assassinating Jews considered to be in collusion with the Romans. On this view, Judas initially followed Jesus because he believed he would be the warrior messiah who would liberate Israel from foreign domination. When it became clear that Jesus would not live up to these hopes, Judas betrayed him to the authorities out of disillusionment.

But why would it take so long for Judas to figure out that Jesus was not an advocate of armed revolt? From the very first words of the Sermon on the Mount to the very first parables of kingdom, Jesus made clear that his way repudiated violence. His was a consistent rejection of domination in all its forms. Judas could scarcely have missed the point of everything Jesus had said. It is true that the disciples are depicted as extraordinarily obtuse on this subject. Does Jesus give Judas one of the places of honor at the feast because he is trying one last time to win him over to his way? This much seems to be true: Judas was disappointed in Jesus and decided to do something about it.

Least convincing of all is the theory that Judas betrayed Jesus hoping it would provoke Jesus to fight. If that were the case, Judas would not have taken Jesus and his disciples by surprise but would have made sure that they had every advantage in numbers, weapons, location, and surprise: a hundred men, armed to the teeth, hiding in a gulch, with Judas signaling the attack with his own sicarius (dagger)!

No, Judas supplied the authorities with precisely what they had been seeking: someone in the inner circle who could lead them to the place where Jesus and his disciples were bivouacked on the Mount of Olives, by night, when the temple crowds could not intervene. Had Judas been a revolutionary, he would surely have played the crowds to the limit.

3. There is a third theory, also held by John's Gospel but shared as well by Luke: Satan had entered into Judas. Curiously, modern commentators have had very little interest in this option, preferring political, psychological, or characterological explanations. But the theological explanation deserves serious consideration. If we suspend

traditional depictions of Satan as a metaphysical person of evil intent, and think of Satan instead as the *spirit of the Domination System,* then this theory makes instant sense: Judas let himself be seized, or possessed, by the very Powers Jesus was opposing. "Then Satan entered into Judas called Iscariot": Here it becomes possible to combine elements of some of the earlier theories. Perhaps Judas had been an assassin and, in frustration and rage at Jesus' failure to do anything about the Romans and their Jewish lackeys, fell back into his old reliance on violence as the cure for violence.

But why then did Judas not kill Jesus himself? Or just quit the movement? Jesus was doing no positive harm to the cause, such that he needed to be removed. Why place him in the very hands of the people Judas himself most hated? Why would Judas deal with his greatest enemies? Why identify him with a kiss rather than simply point his finger? He could have been arrested a hundred other ways. Why this way?

We must finally conclude that no theory is adequate to explain so deep a betrayal. There is finally no "reason" for it, any more than there is an explanation for our betrayals of one another and the gospel. We have every reason not to betray, yet we do so. Betrayal is one of the darkest, most confounding mysteries in the life of the spirit. Why does one of his own inner circle, one of his closest associates, betray Jesus? How is darkness able to abide so close to the light?

The kiss is the most devastating. It is not merely the kiss of greeting (*phileo,* v. 48) but a passionate or effusive kiss (the intensive, *kataphileo,* v. 49), the kind of kiss given by the father to the prodigal on his return (Luke 15:20) or the farewell given Paul by friends who knew they would never see him again (Acts 20:37). There is no suggestion of homosexuality here. This kiss is not a pretense of love. It is choked with fury and rage. What we are dealing with is a hatred of the light that comes, not from opponents of the light, but from one who has seen the light, embraced the light, and suddenly, in a volcanic reversal, knowingly repudiates the light.

In the world's myths, a kiss awakens sleepers, frees them from enchantment, or breaks a curse. That is what makes this kiss so diabolical: It is a kiss to kill, to curse, to annihilate. What does it do to the soul to call on the powers of darkness to annihilate what one loves? "Satan entered into Judas," and Jesus enters into night. "This is your hour, and the power of darkness," Jesus tells Judas and the arresting party (Luke 22:53). "And it was night," says the Fourth Gospel as Judas leaves the feast (13:30).

This terrible, unthinkable kiss, this horrible linkage of orifices that blasphemes love: Is this Judas's desperate bolt toward linkage, whereby

he brings to Jesus his own darkness and dumps it on him, refusing to claim it as his own? Is this finally the only way Judas can find to deal with his own unacceptable darkness: to project it all on Jesus and then engineer its destruction in him? Possessed by the spirit of domination, unable to acknowledge that he was, at heart, *no different in kind from the Romans,* has Judas succumbed to that satanic spirit and turned against the man who threatened an end to domination—including the counterviolence of the oppressed?

Is it then the case that the closer we get to the self, the more the darkness is constellated? That betrayal and intimacy always belong together? That increased consciousness does not make us more invulnerable, but rather the opposite: more vulnerable, fragile, receptive, permeable? Can we then state it as a truth that the more one constellates the highest value, the more one constellates the darkness? Consciousness is the most improbable state in nature, and the greater the consciousness, the greater the pull of entropy. Judas represents the part of us that would sooner destroy the universe than submit to fundamental transformation in the self.

Every advance in justice is met by counterresistance from the Powers that stand to lose from a more equitable system. There is no such thing as linear progress, with evil gradually decreasing as the good augments. What we have instead resembles lurches and pullbacks in fits and starts. The women's suffrage movement was halted by World War I on the basis of patriotic appeals for a united front. It took almost fifty years to restore the momentum. Now women's most recent gains are being challenged by a powerful backlash.

Judas is able, in a horrifying way, to further the destiny of Jesus, but not his own. The truth evokes not joy in him but a frantic attempt to crush the teller. Having projected his own evil on Jesus in such a way that Jesus had to be destroyed, Judas was unable to take his own darkness back and deal with it; hence his suicide was a logical consequence of letting that aspect of himself die with Jesus. But one must also say that he still could have been redeemed had he only turned in time. The one who died for the ungodly (Rom. 5:6) also died for Judas. What if, instead of hanging himself, he had gone back and faced the community with what he had done?

Perhaps this sheds light on why Jesus kept Judas in his intimate circle. This was perhaps the ultimate demonstration of loving enemies. To the very end Jesus holds Judas in the light, placing him on his left side at the final supper. It is to Judas, too, that Jesus gives the bread of life and the cup of salvation, which Matthew declares to be for "the forgiveness of sins" (26:28). When it becomes clear that Judas has chosen night, Jesus does nothing to stop him. As the arresting party arrives, according to Matthew, Jesus calls Judas "friend" (26:50). Even if the narratives as we have them are to a degree the result of later reflection, this detail about Judas on Jesus' left is not representative of the church's trajectory of reflection, in which feelings of hatred increasingly dominate the narrative.

Thus Luke pronounces a woe on Judas, equivalent to a curse (Luke 22:22), and in Acts 1:15-20 says Judas bought a field with the reward of his wickedness (Luke omits the thirty pieces of silver that his sources included and lets the reader assume that his reward was a considerable sum). "And falling headlong, he burst open in the middle and all his bowels gushed out." Does this encourage you to believe that the early church would have forgiven him? It was one thing for the Fourth Gospel to say that "the devil had already put it into the heart of Judas" to betray Jesus (13:2), but another thing altogether to *identify* him without remainder as "a devil" (6:70). It would appear that Satan entered into several other hearts as well, to make them demonize Judas.

But we cannot so easily dismiss Judas. We know him too intimately within. Can you name the part of you that could betray the things you hold dearest—with a kiss? How have you betrayed others? How have you been betrayed? Betrayal of friendships, betrayal of spouses, betrayal of children, betrayal of trust, betrayal of professional relationships: Judas is all too real to us. How we love to hate him, distancing our own inner darkness by dumping it all on him, just as he dumped his on Jesus. Thus we continue the spiral of betrayals as we hide from the Judas within.

In a remarkable play, *A Very Cold Night,* by Dennis Winnie, Jesus appears to Judas in hell, still seeking to win him. There is something infinitely true here. Perhaps there can be no salvation as long as Judas is not saved. There is certainly no salvation until the Judas within us is saved. For, much as we would like to avoid them, betrayal and being betrayed are an inevitable part of the journey to wholeness. It is the darkness nearest the center, and we must pass through that darkness to reach our goal, whether we like it or not.

Just as Jesus did.

Maundy Thursday

Lutheran	Roman Catholic	Episcopal	Common Lectionary
Exod. 24:3-11	Exod. 12:1-8, 11-14	Exod. 12:1-14a	Exod. 12:1-14 or Exod. 24:3-8
1 Cor. 10:16-17	1 Cor. 11:23-26	1 Cor. 11:23-26 (27-32)	1 Cor. 11:23-26 or 1 Cor. 10:16-17
Mark 14:12-26	John 13:1-15	John 13:1-15 or Luke 22:14-30	John 13:1-15 or Mark 14:12-26

FIRST LESSON: EXODUS 12:1-14; 24:3-11

Exodus 12:1-14 recounts the institution of the Passover meal as Israel prepared itself to escape from bondage in Egypt. The narrative has the appearance of an oil painting repeatedly revised to make room for new developments, with all the stages of evolution showing through. The occasion of the Exodus is the basis of a new calendar (12:2); this may reflect postexilic practice. Special allowances are made for small households to join their closest neighbors in sharing a lamb together (12:4). Later sacrificial scrupulosities are introduced to insure that the lambs offered are one-year-old males without blemish—a detail not likely to have preoccupied Israelites force-feeding themselves in haste, standing, fully clothed for flight. Nor would "the whole assembled congregation of Israel" have gathered for the slaughtering of all these lambs if they were trying to keep their flight secret; this reflects rather the developed cultus in the Jerusalem temple. And of course the fleeing Israelites were not ordered to eat the lamb with bitter herbs and specially made unleavened bread; they simply ate what they had, and the bread had no time to rise, such was their haste. No doubt the Israelites saw their deliverance as a victory of this strange new god Yahweh over the local Egyptian deities (Exod. 12:12), but it is probably later theological reflection that saw the exodus as primarily a religious affair.

In short, like the narratives that institute the Eucharist (see below), the Passover traditions have evolved, becoming cultic and liturgical. That is the proper function of memory: to preserve, through ritual, the breakthrough experiences of a people when it discovered its own identity in God. Once they were no people; now they are a people, because they have been constituted by common experience, common commitment, common vocation.

Whatever its similarities with the festal meals of other peoples, Israel's Passover was like nothing the world had seen since the rise of the conquest states around 3000 B.C.E. Now, at last, the ultimate principle of the universe was perceived no longer as the parent of the king but the champion of the dispossessed. The spiritual reality at the center of every living being was now seen to be in solidarity, not with aristocrats, but slaves. Justice, not power, was installed as the highest value, and compassion was elevated over might. Every other "civilized" nation, tongue, tribe, and people had told the story of reality from the top down: first divine beings, then kings, priests, warriors, artisans, and, at the bottom, peasants. Statecraft was a matter of control, of order, of domination of the many by the few in a pyramid of powers. To tell the story of reality from below was without precedent in all of ancient history.

Passover could not simply be memorialized as a founding event of the Jewish people, therefore. It had to become the foundation of Jewish consciousness as a people. Even for those tribes who were not in Egypt, who would later unite with Israel; even for those born later in time, who had not participated in that originative event: This story had to become their story. Not just in biology but in the realm of the spirit, the rule applies: Ontogeny recapitulates phylogeny. Just as the individual being recapitulates the entire evolution of the human race in its mother's womb (developing gill slits, a tail stub, then reabsorbing them), so each new generation must also recapitulate and internalize the entire spiritual evolution of its community of belief.

Thus in the Passover celebration, each participant recites, "A wandering Aramean was *my* ancestor; he went down into Egypt and lived there as an alien. . . . When the Egyptians treated *us* harshly and afflicted *us*, . . . *we* cried to the Lord, the God of our ancestors; the Lord heard *our* voice and saw *our* affliction, *our* toil, and *our* oppression. The Lord brought *us* out of Egypt with a mighty hand and an outstretched arm, . . . and he brought *us* into this place and gave *us* this land, a land flowing with milk and honey" (Deut. 26:5-9). One does not become a Jew simply by being born a Jew. One must take on the entire history of the Jewish people, from its inception, creatively living it forward into the future.

In his temptation in the wilderness, Jesus is depicted as *recapitulating* the history of his people. Satan's strategy is to deceive him into *repetition,* whereby one attempts to perpetuate the past rather than living it forward. Satan thus tries to lure Jesus into becoming a second Moses or a second David rather than the first Jesus. But Jesus also rejects the temptation of launching out on his own, free of the tradition altogether. He charts his course by means of an exegesis of Deuteronomy.

One of the dangers of the new spirituality in modern Western culture, despite its many authentic contributions, is that people are tempted to flit from flower to flower, to suck up whatever nectar that can be had without struggle, and then to dart off to another guru or another spiritual technology or psychic magician as soon as the going gets tough. It seems to be the case that true spiritual profundity is found only by going deeply into a single tradition, though remaining open to truth wherever it can be found. As Saint Gregory of Sinai put it, "Trees that are repeatedly transplanted do not grow roots."

Patterns of behavior have to be learned. Disciplines must be mastered. An individual must therefore be initiated into the wisdom of the past; it is too vast to be sorted through alone, and too elusive to be redis-covered by each new generation. Long before the age of choice, we find our identity by means of imitation, incorporation into a tradition, and solidarity with a group of people. Circumcision and Passover, Baptism and Eucharist: These are more than membership rites. They are constitutive of the spiritual identity of those who are sojourners toward God's domination-free order.

Exodus 24:3-8 is an early piece of tradition framed by 24:1-2 and 9-11, which have been separated in order to make the cultic meal with God the climax of the covenantal act. This scene is made the focus of Heb. 9:18-21. But in Exodus 24, as Brevard Childs notes, the blood was only part of the ceremony of ratification and did not function to forgive sins (*The Book of Exodus,* Old Testament Library [Philadelphia: Westminster Press, 1974], 511). In Hebrews, by contrast, the writer has transformed the ceremony into a ritual in which the entire emphasis now falls on the forgiveness of sins through the shedding of blood: "Indeed, under the law almost everything is purified with blood, and without the shedding of blood there is no forgiveness of sins" (Heb. 9:22).

But Jesus, as remarked before, freely forgave sins during his ministry, solely on the basis of his new perception of the nature of God. The function of the blood in the ratification ceremony of Exodus is to underline the costliness of the covenant. The blood of the animal stands in place of the blood of the people. They are dashed with the blood to incriminate them in the animal's killing or as evidence of their compliance and participation. The blood stands as a threat against them if they fail to live up to the terms of the covenant: blood for blood if they fail. Forgiveness is not the point here, because they were not enslaved in Egypt because of their sins. They were liberated precisely because of their neediness, their lack of a champion, their cries to heaven for a God who would side with the poor. Their sins in the wilderness had to do with their reverting to earlier behaviors: Egyptian mores, Egyptian idolatry, and the mentality of slaves. In setting them free, then, Yahweh does not cleanse them of personal sins so much as of collective socialization in the ethos of domination.

When Hebrews shifts the focus to a personal forgiveness that opens the way to eternal life in a Platonic, otherworldly heaven, it ignores the task of overcoming the Domination System. The author is not unaware of that system; chapters 10–13 chronicle the sufferings that faith has brought upon the early Christians in the context of a hostile empire. But the emphasis now resides elsewhere, not in a world redeemed but another, nonmaterial world altogether. The church has never fully recovered from that shift.

SECOND LESSON: 1 CORINTHIANS 10:16-17; 11:23-26

Unlike Hebrews, which turns back to the old metaphor of sacrifice to explain the death of Jesus, Paul mints a new metaphor: the body of Christ. "The cup of blessing that we bless, is it not a sharing in the blood of Christ? The bread that we break, is it not a sharing in the body of Christ? Because there is one bread, we who are many are one body, for we all partake of the one bread" (1 Cor. 10:16-17). The image is organic. Jesus' act of offering himself in order to reconcile us to God entails giving us his very body and blood to eat. By so doing we are incorporated into his living body, the church, a new superorganism, the next stage in human evolution. This new body is to be a foretaste of what the whole world will become when God wins the final victory over domination and death.

But sharing in the blood of Christ means that we will also suffer with Christ as a world of dominations enforced by death sniffs the aroma of that new reality and attempts to destroy it by every available means. Being incorporated into that body also has implications for practical ethics. First Corinthians 10:16-17 is embedded not in a discussion of the Eucharist but in a disquisition on idolatry, sexual morality, and eating meat sacrificed to idols (10:6-22). Incarnating God in our bodies has consequences for our behavior in our bodies. Jesus' sacrifice, after all, was not in order to elevate us, unchanged, into a superstratospheric heaven. It was to liberate us from patterns, habits, obsessions, and addictions so that we might more fully become the people God created us to be, here, now, even under the conditions of the old order.

GOSPEL: MARK 14:12-26; JOHN 13:1-15; LUKE 22:14-30

Many scholars believe that Luke had a special source for the passion narrative, beginning at Luke 22:14, which he prefers to Mark. In Luke's account of the last supper, Jesus tells his disciples how earnestly he had desired to eat the Passover with them before his arrest and execution. But now, he vows, he will abstain until it is fulfilled in God's domination-free order that is coming. Likewise, in one of the four blessings over the cup that characterized the Passover meal, Jesus gives the wine to his disciples and tells them to divide it among themselves, again apparently abstaining: "For I tell you that from now on I will not drink of the fruit of the vine until the kingdom of God comes." Why, according to Luke's special source, is Jesus fasting during the Passover meal?

How can he eat the Passover meal if he himself is not going to be "passed over" by the angel of death? This, the firstborn of many brothers and sisters (Rom. 8:29), is, like the firstborn of Egypt, unprotected by the blood of the paschal lamb. Passed over in the slaughter of the innocents in Matthew's infancy account, he will not be passed over now. The Powers have spread their net for him; the betrayer is at his very table. The wheel that will crush him is already grinding toward him, and by choosing not to flee, Jesus voluntarily, deliberately, hurls himself into its path. He now has a date with the angel of death, and so he abstains from the meal.

Perhaps, too, he vows to fast until the reign of God dawns in order to hasten its coming. Does he still harbor the hope that the new order might burst in on the world before his death? Is he clinging desperately to the hope that God might still find a less painful way? In Gethsemane he reminds God that all things are possible to God. And many things are still possible. Judas might repent; Jesus' special regard for him at the supper keeps that possibility open. The authorities might not be able to find a suitable charge; they do, in fact, have difficulty finding witnesses who agree. Pilate might show a little spine, since the charges are technically trivial (although Jesus is indeed the ultimate threat to the System of Domination of which Pilate is the local representative). Angels might intervene, if in fact the world is so ordered (which I doubt). The crowd might shout for the release of Jesus rather than Barabbas.

But not everything is still possible for God. Not if Jesus refuses to flee. Not if he remains faithful to his own integrity. Not if he continues to expose the illegitimacy of all those persons and Powers that have organized the world in defiance of the intent of God. God is constrained by the free choice of Jesus to hold fast to who he is, and by the free choice of the Powers to obliterate him. Imagine the horror of God, helpless to intervene to prevent the inevitable collision.

Again, Jesus cannot eat and drink at the last supper because he identifies the bread and the wine as his own body and blood. How can he then devour himself? As the symbols of a new covenant, however, bread and wine will serve to unite the disciples with him in one body, one mission, one divine objective for the transformation of the planet. They will become his body, and continue his life in the world. So he abstains from the meal, offering himself as it chief substance. This meal will then function to unite his followers into a new society, a new covenant, a new body capable of incarnating God's new order.

Jesus refuses to be caught in repetition of the Passover rite. He transforms it by a fresh recapitulation. He finds himself in that narrative, not, however, as the faithful descendants who identify with their oppressed forebears, but as the firstborn who will not be saved by blood from the angel of death. He thus recasts the story. He restages the drama so as to include the present crisis. The political event of liberation from Egypt becomes the lens through which he finds meaning and orientation in the face of the plot against his life. He uses the tradition creatively, adjusting it to fit the changed circumstances and needs of the present and interpreting the opacity of the present moment through the rich resources of the tradition.

The early church exercised the same sovereign freedom with the last supper. The Synoptic Gospels portray a full-scale Passover supper, with lamb, bitter and green herbs, a sauce of fruit puree, unleavened bread, and four cups of wine. When the gospel passed into gentile lands, however, the Passover ritual was both alien and meaningless. So the gentile churches transformed the last supper into a mystery rite, following the pattern of mystery religions long known in their regions. The accounts of the last supper in Matthew, Mark, and 1 Corinthians (and Luke 22:19-20, whatever its textual history) focus no longer on the meal but only on the two elements, bread and wine. Not the continuation of his ministry but Jesus' own body and being become the locus of devotion. The Jewish past is put at a distance by being titled the "old covenant" and distinguished from and superseded by the new. Now, instead of everyone being welcome, as at Jesus' other meals, the last supper becomes a mystery rite available only to initiates or members. Now Jesus presides over the meal like a priest and eats the meal with them. The last supper becomes the first Eucharist, which now marks the institution of the Christian religion as an entity separate from Judaism. The bread and wine now supernaturally transubstantiate; they are not symbols but the real presence of Christ.

Further changes took place in the medieval, Reformation, and post-Reformation churches. Enough has been said, however, to indicate that true transmission of a tradition means changing it, adapting it to current needs without abandoning its links to its original impulse. Tradition can also serve to critique current practice. The Bible can provide fresh possibilities for interpretation and liturgical development.

Perhaps the most appalling defection from Jesus' original impulse is the way the Eucharist has been reserved only for baptized Christians and, often, only members of a particular denomination. Disputes over the Eucharist have been the primary cause of division between various wings of Christianity. Vast numbers of Christians are refused access to the Lord's table in denominations other than their own. Nowhere is the church of Jesus Christ more out of touch with the spirit of Jesus than in the way we conduct and closet the Eucharist.

Nothing was so radical and unprecedented as the way Jesus treated meals. Rather than surrounding himself with like-minded religious figures, he ate with tax collectors and sinners (Mark 2:15-17 par.). He accepted an invitation to a Pharisee's house for a banquet, but then, when a woman burst in and began to kiss his feet, wet them with her tears, wipe them with her hair, and anoint them with oil, Jesus takes her side, despite the sharp censure of the others at table (Luke 7:36-50). His love of dining earned him the Falstaffian reputation of "a glutton and a drunkard, a friend of tax collectors and sinners!" (Matt. 11:19; Luke 7:34). Virtually the only concrete image he provides of what the reign of God will be like is that of a banquet (Matt. 22:1-10//Luke 14:15-24; Matt. 8:11-12//Luke 13:28-30; Luke 22:28-30). As a foretaste of that coming feast, he feeds the five thousand in the wilderness (Mark 6:30-44). He presses on his hearers a whole new school of etiquette: When invited to a banquet, observe the protocol of God's nonhierarchical order and take the lowest seat. If you are giving a banquet, invite not those with status and prestige but the poor, the maimed, the lame, and the blind (Luke 14:7-14). So topsy-turvy are the values of this new order that a master will cause his slaves to recline on the festal couch and serve them a meal himself (Luke 12:37)!

After his death, Jesus is made known to them not through exegesis of prophecies but in his most characteristic act among them: the blessing and breaking of bread (Luke 24:13-35). He proves to doubters that he is risen by demonstrating once more his voracious appetite (Luke 24:41-43). When he appears to the disciples beside the sea, he identifies himself by offering a fish-fry (John 21:1-14).

When the early church sought to remain faithful to his way, they could do nothing better than continue his meals (Acts 2:42-47; 6:1-6; 10:1—11:18; 1 Cor. 11:17-22, 33-34). They were not locked into a fixed form. In the Pseudo-Clementine writings they shared bread, water, and salt, the typical meal of the impoverished. The catacomb paintings most frequently depict bread and fish. In short, they used whatever they had as their normal fare to celebrate their agape meals.

The last supper must be seen in the broad sweep of Jesus' meals. It was but one among all the dinners he shared as an anticipation and installment of the reign of God. And what was most remarkable about these meals was that *everyone was invited*. With his meals, Jesus broke down the barrier between rich and poor, ins and outs, righteous and sinner, clean and unclean. The church would later add Jew and Gentile. Here was a new reality where men and women ate together, where master and slave, teacher and disciple, old and young were all on the same level. It was precisely the obliteration of the walls of distinction that marked the new dispensation. In that spirit the Fourth Gospel depicts Jesus washing the disciples' feet—an unthinkable act for a teacher—as the centerpiece of the last supper (13:1-15).

So when we today perpetuate the Eucharist as a mystery rite closed to outsiders, we utterly violate the spirit of Jesus. Rather than welcoming only baptized Christians, or even more narrowly, card-carrying members of our particular sect, we should be holding meals and inviting the poor, the homeless, recently released convicts, families below the poverty line. *This is precisely what some churches are doing.* But instead of calling it an agape, we call it a soup kitchen. Rather than seeing that it is here that the living presence of Jesus is most clearly known, we "operate" these charity dinners as a kind of "good works," then go upstairs to the chancel to receive the "real" Eucharist.

But Jesus is where he has always been, among the poor. Forget doctrine. His presence is nowhere more real than when people share their food with others who hunger for the real presence: of God, of Jesus, of ourselves.

Perhaps, then, if we were to exercise the same sovereign freedom with our tradition that Jesus and his followers have through the centuries, we would fast on Maundy Thursday and refuse to take the Eucharist if it is offered only to baptized Christians. Maybe the spectacle of Christians going forward for the bread and wine and then abstaining would awaken others to the travesty of turning Jesus' wide open meals for everyone into a closed sacrament.

Good Friday

Lutheran	Roman Catholic	Episcopal	Common Lectionary
Isa. 52:13—53:12	Isa. 52:13—53:12	Isa. 52:13—53:12 *or* Gen. 22:1-18 *or* Wis. 2:1, 12-24	Isa. 52:13—53:12
Heb. 4:14-16; 5:7-9	Heb. 4:14-16; 5:7-9	Heb. 10:1-25	Heb. 4:14-16; 5:7-9
John 18:1—19:42	John 18:1—19:42	John 18:1—19:42 *or* 19:1-37	John 18:1—19:42 *or* 19:17-30

FIRST LESSON: ISAIAH 52:13—53:12

This is the fourth song of the Servant of the Lord. The Revised English Bible translates it brilliantly.

It is virtually impossible for a Christian not to see in this song a complete prefigurement of the crucifixion of Jesus. Already in the days of Second Isaiah, almost six hundred years before Jesus, God was apparently doing a new thing that would "prepare the way of the Lord" (Isa. 40:3). The writer acknowledges that the prophetic message is unbelievable, and that the kind of divine power that is about to be revealed is unthinkable (53:1). God is hereby revealing the secret hidden from the foundation of the world: the scapegoat mechanism.

In a series of studies that may well constitute one of the more important contributions to thought in this century, René Girard has laid bare the dynamics of scapegoating. (See his *The Scapegoat* [Baltimore: John Hopkins University Press, 1986], and *Things Hidden from the Foundation of the World* [Stanford: Stanford University Press, 1987].) Human beings, lacking the instinctual braking mechanisms that cause a wolf to spare its defeated rival, fell headlong into endless spirals of ever-escalating retaliation. Those societies that survived did so, Girard believes, because they discovered a mechanism by which all parties could perform a "final" killing of a surrogate victim. This "scapegoat," usually randomly chosen, disabled, odd, or marginal, has to be someone whose death or expulsion no one will seek to avenge and who everyone can agree is to blame for the conflict. The scapegoat is regarded, on the one hand, as odious, monstrous, an object of hatred and contempt:

> Many were appalled, . . . many nations recoil at the sight of him, and kings curl their lips in disgust. His form, disfigured, lost all human likeness; his appearance so changed he no longer looked like a man. (Isa. 52:14-15, REB)

> He grew up before the Lord like a young plant whose roots are in parched ground; he had no beauty, no majesty to catch our eyes, no grace to attract us to him. He was despised, shunned by all, pain-racked and afflicted by disease; we despised him, we held him of no account, an object from which people turn away their eyes. (53:2-3, REB)

Yet, because the scapegoat's death brings reconciliation to the quarreling parties, he or she is often regarded as a savior, a god, or a cult figure.

> Yet it was our afflictions he was bearing, our pain he endured, while we thought of him as smitten by God, struck down by disease and misery. But he was pierced for our transgressions, crushed for our iniquities; the chastisement he bore restored us to health and by his wounds we are healed. (53:4-5, REB)

So far nothing here is exceptional. This is the way human societies from time immemorial have learned to defuse violence. Herein lies the origin, Girard argues, of the gods, of religion, of sacrifice, of ritual, of myth.

Traditionally the victim was taken to the edge of a cliff. The entire community formed a half-circle and began to hurl stones. Thus everyone, and no one, was guilty of his death. Having removed this threat, and having celebrated the reconciliation that the scapegoat made possible, the community was restored to peace.

Myth arises to obscure the murderous nature of scapegoating by providing a fictional account of the event, says Girard. The arbitrariness of the victim's murder is covered by declaring it a divine necessity. The gods thus created by humanity demand the death of victims. But the hunger for blood projected onto the gods is in fact a metaphysical howling instituted by the murderers to drown out the cry rising from innocent blood spilled on the ground.

So powerful is the collective trance, so mesmerizing the dances, costumes, pageantry, and drumbeats of the ritual, that the victims may even offer themselves to immolation willingly, like the Aztec maidens or the victims of Stalin's purges. The group thus splits off its violence from consciousness and transfers it not to the unconscious but to religious or quasi-religious political institutions.

> He was maltreated, yet he was submissive and did not open his mouth; like a sheep led to the slaughter, like a ewe that is dumb before the shearers, he did not open his mouth. He was arrested and sentenced and taken away, and who gave a thought to his fate—how he was cut off from the world of the living, stricken to death for my people's transgression? (53:7-8, REB)

The scapegoat mechanism is characterized by the following elements:

1. *Mimetic desire.* We become human, in large part, by learning from others what to desire and then copying them. We imitate them (mimesis) by desiring what they desire. Such desire is in itself good. We learn by mimicry what is a good worth striving for. Value is defined for us as that which someone we admire wants.

2. *Mimetic rivalry.* But in a world of scarcity, mimetic desire issues in a double bind: The one imitated says, "Be like me. Value this object." But when the imitator reaches out to take it, rivalry occurs, and the one imitated says, "Do not be like me. It's mine." Conflict inevitably ensues from mimetic desire, because both parties now competitively desire the same thing. The rival, who once modeled behavior, becomes the object of hostility and possibly violence.

3. *The crisis of distinctions.* When the differences that formerly separated potential rivals are dissolved as a result of their both desiring the same thing, the social distinctions by which order was preserved collapse. Girard calls this a crisis of distinctions. Students seize the administration building and demand a share in decision-making power that has previously been the sole prerogative of the administrators. Mill workers shut down the plant and insist on a voice in shaping their new contract. The hierarchical barriers that society has so carefully erected, unjust as they may be, dike society against the flood of anarchy. When these distinctions collapse (as when soldiers in Vietnam refused to obey orders from their officers), that social system faces the possibility of collapse. Collapse can be averted, however, if society can find a scapegoat.

4. *The necessary victim.* The scapegoat can be a foreigner, an eccentric, a communist (or someone labeled communist), a witch, a carrier of the plague, a homosexual, a purveyor of new ideas, a prophet—in any case, his or her murder resolves the crisis. The fiction of the scapegoat's guilt must be maintained regardless of the real truth of the matter. The fact that hostilities cease following the scapegoat's death seems to confirm that he or she indeed was their cause and that therefore the execution was justified. The key is the doctrine of Caiaphas: It is expedient that one person die and that the whole nation not perish (John 11:50; 18:14). The group discharges its violence on the scapegoat and can now redirect its energies into mutual cooperation, even reconciliation.

5. *Sacralizing the victim.* The necessary victim is rendered sacred by being simultaneously regarded as accursed and life-bringing. As compensation for his or her sacrificial death, the victim is endowed with special honors and sometimes even elevated to divinity. Not only can

violence now be survived, it has provided the impetus for the development of religious ritual and myth, and, through their generative influence, legislation and human culture.

6. *Sacrificial repetition.* Subsequent sacrifices repeat in strictly controlled ritual the primordial structure of the scapegoat mechanism. Internal aggressions are thus diverted and expended ritually, and the social fabric is preserved.

Religion is therefore, according to Girard, organized violence in the service of social tranquillity. Religion covers up the sacrificial mechanism by means of myth, ritual, and prohibition. It institutionalizes amnesia regarding the origins of violence and endows violence with an aura of necessity and divine ordination, which disguises its cost to the victims. Religious systems cannot permit their violence to be known, even to themselves. In *Fear and Trembling,* Søren Kierkegaard identified this obfuscation with characteristic clarity: "The ethical expression for what Abraham did is, that he would murder Isaac; the religious expression is, that he would sacrifice Isaac." By means of ritual, religion substitutes an animal for the original victim. By means of myth it conceals the original violent murder while still maintaining an invisible connection to its life-giving power. And by elevating the victim to the status of a god, it erases remorse for his slaughter.

There is in the universe, however, a counterforce to the power of myth, ritual, and religion, says Girard, one that exposes the immortal lie for what it is, and that is the Christian gospel. Girard understands the Hebrew Bible as a long and laborious exodus out of the world of violence and sacred projections, an exodus plagued by many reversals, and one that fell short of its goal. The mechanics of violence and projection remain partly hidden. The old sacred notions are never quite exposed in their true meaning, despite the process of revelation. Nevertheless, here, and only here, is that process begun.

The violence of the Old Testament has always been a scandal to Christianity. The church has usually ducked the issue, by avoidance, allegorizing, Marcionism, or special pleading. In his Girardian meditation *Must There Be Scapegoats?* (San Francisco: Harper & Row, 1987), Raymund Schwager points out that there are six hundred passages of explicit violence in the Hebrew Bible, one thousand verses where God's own violent actions of punishment are described, a hundred passages where Yahweh expressly commands others to kill people, and several stories where God irrationally kills or tries to kill for no apparent reason (e.g., Exod. 4:24-26). Violence, Schwager concludes, is easily the most often mentioned activity and central theme of the Hebrew Bible.

This violence is in part the residue of false ideas about God carried over from the general human past. It is also, however, the beginning of a process of raising the scapegoating mechanism to consciousness, so that these projections on God can be withdrawn. Now, for the first time in all of human history, God begins to be seen as identified with the *victims* of violence. All other myths, Girard says, have been written from the point of view of the victimizers. But Scripture rehabilitates persecuted sufferers. God is revealed, not as demanding sacrifice, but as taking the part of the sacrificed. From Genesis to Revelation, the victims cry for justice and deliverance from the world of myth where they are made scapegoats. In the cross these cries find vindication. But these occasional critiques of domination in the Hebrew Bible continue to coexist with texts that call on Israel to exterminate its enemies now or in the last days (Micah 4:13; Joel 3:1-21).

In the Hebrew Bible, with only a few exceptions that are all legendary, whenever God acts to punish, God does so through human beings attacking one another. This indicates, says Schwager, that the actual initiative for killing does not originate in God but is projected onto God by those who desire revenge. Yahweh's followers projected their own jealousy onto God and made God as jealous as they. But something new emerges nonetheless: Yahweh openly insists on this jealousy, which begins to reveal Yahweh's singular relationship to Israel as one of love.

The violence of the Bible is the necessary precondition for the gradual perception of its meaning. The scapegoat mechanism could not have come to consciousness in a nonviolent society. The problem of violence could emerge only at the very heart of violence, in the most war-ravaged corridor on the globe, by a repeatedly subjugated people unable to seize and wield power for any length of time. The violence of Scripture, so embarrassing to us today, became the means by which sacred violence was revealed for what it is: a lie perpetrated against victims in the name of a God who, through violence, was working to expose violence for what it is and to reveal the divine nature as nonviolent.

We see that exposure in God's intervention to stop Abraham's sacrifice of Isaac and in the exodus. But nowhere is it articulated more clearly in the Hebrew Scriptures than in Isaiah 53. The great historic turning point begins in 53:9. Until now this sacrificial death has been routine, a perfectly normal scapegoating procedure moving toward its inevitable conclusion. But what is this? The scapegoat is openly declared to be innocent!

> He was assigned a grave with the wicked, a burial-place among felons, *though he had done no violence, had spoken no word of treachery.* (53:9, REB)

More wonderful yet, God intervenes on the side of the scapegoat!

> Yet the Lord took thought for his oppressed servant and healed him who had given himself as a sacrifice for sin. (53:10a, REB)

God vindicates the servant by what can only be resurrection, restoring him, apparently, to earthly life:

> He will enjoy long life and see his children's children, and in his hand the Lord's purpose will prosper. (53:10b, REB)

Not only that, but the servant's agony will issue not just in the temporary truce gained by the scapegoat but in genuine salvation:

> By his humiliation my servant will justify many; after his suffering he will see light and be satisfied; it is their guilt he bears. Therefore I shall allot him a portion with the great, and he will share the spoil with the mighty, because he exposed himself to death and was reckoned among transgressors, for he bore the sin of many and interceded for transgressors. (53:11-12, REB)

SECOND LESSON: HEBREWS 4:14-16; 5:7-9

What Second Isaiah saw with such prescience is actually lived out by Jesus. In his passion and death, the scapegoat mechanism is fully exposed and revoked.

There is nothing unique about the death of Jesus: his sufferings, his persecution, his being scapegoated. Nor is there anything unique about the coalition of all the worldly powers intent that one man should die for the people so that the nation should not be destroyed (John 11:50). What is astonishing, says Girard, is that contrary to all mythological, political, and philosophical texts, the gospel denounces the verdict passed by these Powers as a total miscarriage of justice, a perfect example of untruth, a crime against God. The Gospels are at great pains to show that the charges against Jesus do not hold water, not in order to avoid suspicion of subversion, but precisely to reveal the scapegoating mechanism. The enemy of the state and of religion is, in fact, an innocent victim.

> In the days of his flesh, Jesus offered up prayers and supplications, with loud cries and tears, to the one who was able to save him from death, and he was heard because of his reverent submission. Although he was a Son, he learned obedience through what he suffered. (Heb. 5:7-8)

It is precisely his obedient submission to unjust suffering that has qualified him as a "high priest according to the order of Melchizedek" (Heb. 5:10). The very Powers that sought to obliterate him discovered instead that they had merely multiplied his efficacy. His death, once and for all, ends all need for further sacrificing forever (Heb. 7:27).

The scapegoating mechanism has now, definitively, been exposed for what it is: a travesty performed in the name of God.

GOSPEL: JOHN 18:1—19:42

Jesus never succumbed to the perspective of the persecutors —either in a positive way, by openly agreeing with his executioners, or in a negative way, by yielding to vengeance in mimetic repetition of the executioners' crime. In Jesus there is a total absence of positive or negative complicity in violence. His arraignment, trial, crucifixion, and death are different only in that in them the scapegoating mechanism is at last, categorically, revealed for all the world to see. Insofar as other deaths reflect the truth revealed in his dying, they share its integrity and continue its revelation.

The passion narrative in the Gospel of John furthers this revelation by identifying Jesus as the paschal lamb, the "Lamb of God who takes away the sin of the world" (1:29). Thus the chronological differences with the Synoptic Gospels: There the last supper was a Passover meal, and the arrest, trial, and crucifixion took place in the same night and day, Nisan 15. But in John's Gospel, Jesus as paschal lamb must die at the very hour the paschal lambs were slaughtered in the temple. Therefore the events from the last supper through the crucifixion had to take place on Nisan 14, the day before the Passover.

Isaiah 53:7 ("like a lamb that is led to the slaughter") echoes in this identification of Jesus with the paschal lamb. The lamb sacrificed at Passover was not for the removal of sins. It is only when the paschal lamb is amalgamated with the lamb of Isaiah 53 that it becomes an atonement for sins, and this apparently first happened in Christian circles. John did not create that fusion; it is already explicit in 1 Cor. 5:7 and continues to reverberate in Acts 8:32, 1 Pet. 1:19, and Rev. 5:6.

Even the smallest details reflect the paschal motif. Jesus is offered a sponge soaked in cheap sour wine, extended on a branch of hyssop (John 19:29). But hyssop could scarcely produce a branch strong enough and long enough for such a feat; it more likely has been introduced as a symbolic evocation of the blood of the lamb sprinkled by a bunch of hyssop on the lintel and doorposts on Passover night to protect the Israelites from the angel of death (Exod. 12:22). Likewise the emphatic statement that none of his bones were broken (John 19:36) alludes to the requirement that no bone of the paschal lamb should be broken (Exod. 12:46). And the statement "It is finished" means not just that he has finished his course but that the entire system he opposed is also finished, including temple, sacrifice, and cultus (John 19:30).

The Lamb of God that takes away the sin of the world: Can we hear that as if for the first time, as the sacrifice that ends the conspiracy of victimization? From this time forward, the victimizers no longer have cover. They are exposed, unmasked, their lies rendered impotent. This statement, then, is not simply a tired religious claim about some sect's private formula for relieving guilt. It is a statement of fact. This final sacrificial Lamb has stripped from the hands of the masters the scapegoating mechanism. Now they can no longer execute the innocent on the strength of the Caiaphas doctrine that it is better for one person to die than for the whole nation to be destroyed. For that doctrine is in really a demon-god: Moloch of the insatiable appetite. It devours the world. In the gospel message, that travesty is at last exposed. It now has only as much power as people continue to decide to give it.

The Great Vigil of Easter
Saturday of Light

Lutheran	Roman Catholic	Episcopal	Common Lectionary
Gen. 1:1—2:3	Gen. 1:1—2:2	Gen. 1:1—2:2	Gen. 1:1—2:2
Gen. 22:1-18	Gen. 22:1-18	Gen. 22:1-18	Gen. 22:1-18
Exod. 14:10—15:1	Exod. 14:15—15:1	Exod. 14:15—15:1	Exod. 14:15—15:1
Isa. 55:1-11	Isa. 55:1-11	Isa. 55:1-11	Isa. 55:1-11
1 Cor. 15:19-28	Rom. 6:3-11	Rom. 6:3-11	Rom. 6:3-11
Mark 16:1-8	Mark 16:1-7	Matt. 28:1-10	Mark 16:1-8

FIRST LESSON: GENESIS 1:1—2:3

The first creation account is really the second. The earliest, the Yahwist's version, runs from 2:4 through the end of chapter 3. The stately cadences and repeated affirmations of the goodness of creation found in the later creation account—the one in Genesis 1—were composed in exile, during the Babylonian captivity, and are a conscious and deliberate attempt by the "Priestly" writers of the Old Testament to counter the Babylonian myth of creation. It was so successful that few people today have even heard of the Babylonian creation story, while many who have no religious commitment to Judaism or Christianity know the creation myth in Genesis 1. In order to appreciate the Genesis creation story in its original context, we need to understand the Babylonian creation story.

Jesus taught the love of enemies, but Babylonian religion taught their extermination. Violence was, for the religion of ancient Mesopotamia, what love was for Jesus: the central dynamic of existence. The myth that enshrined that culture's sense of life was the *Enuma Elish,* dated to around 1250 B.C.E. in the versions that have survived, but based on traditions considerably older.

In the beginning, according to this myth, Apsu and Tiamat (the sweet and saltwater oceans) bear Mummu (the mist). From them also issue the younger gods, whose frolicking makes so much noise that the elder gods resolve to kill them so they can sleep. This plot of the elder gods is discovered, the younger gods kill Apsu, and his wife Tiamat pledges revenge. The rebel gods in terror turn for salvation to their youngest, Marduk. He exacts a steep price: If he succeeds, he must be given chief and undisputed power in the assembly of the gods. Having extorted this promise, he catches Tiamat in a net, drives an evil wind down her throat, shoots an arrow that bursts her distended belly and pierces her heart; he then splits her skull with a club, and scatters her blood in out-of-the-way places. He stretches out her corpse full length, and from it creates the cosmos.

We are indebted to Paul Ricoeur for his profound commentary on this myth in *The Symbolism of Evil* (1967). He points out that in the Babylonian myth, creation is an act of violence: Tiamat is murdered and dismembered; from her cadaver the world is formed. Order is established by means of disorder. Creation is a violent victory over an enemy older than creation. The origin of evil precedes the origin of things. Chaos (symbolized by Tiamat) is prior to order (represented by Marduk, god of Babylon). Evil is prior to good. Violence inheres in the godhead. Evil is an ineradicable constituent of ultimate reality and possesses ontological priority over good.

The biblical creation story in Genesis 1 is diametrically opposed to all this. There, a good God creates a good creation. Chaos does not resist order. Good is ontologically prior to evil. Neither evil nor violence is a part of the creation, but enter as a result of the first couple's sin and the machinations of the serpent. A basically good reality is thus corrupted by free decisions reached by creatures. In this far more complex and subtle explanation of the origins of things, evil for the first time emerges as a problem requiring solution.

In the Babylonian myth, however, there is no "problem of evil." Evil is simply a primordial fact. The simplicity of its picture of reality commended it widely, and its basic mythic structure spread as far as Syria, Phoenicia, Egypt, Greece, Rome, Germany, Ireland, and India. Typically, a male war god residing in the sky—Wotan, Zeus, or Indra, for example—fights a decisive battle with a female divine being, usually depicted as a monster or dragon, residing in the sea or abyss. Having vanquished the original enemy by war and murder, the victor fashions a cosmos from the monster's corpse. Cosmic order equals the violent suppression of the feminine and is mirrored in the social order by the subjection of women to men. Marduk's accession to supremacy over the gods means at the same time the ascendancy of Babylon over earlier city-states like Nippur and Eridu. Heavenly events are mirrored by earthly events, and what happens above happens below.

After the world has been created, the story continues, the gods imprisoned by Marduk for siding with Tiamat complain of the poor meal service in their jail. Marduk and Ea therefore execute Tiamat's consort, Kingu, and from the blood of this slaughtered god, Ea creates human beings to be servants to the gods.

The implications are clear: Humanity is created from the blood of a murdered god. Our very origin is violence. Killing is in our blood. Humanity is not the originator of evil, but merely finds evil already present and perpetuates it. Our origins are divine, to be sure, since we are made from a god, but from the blood of an assassinated god. We are the consequence of deicide. Human beings are thus naturally incapable of peaceful coexistence; order must continually be imposed upon us from on high. Nor are we created to subdue the earth and have dominion over it as God's regents; we exist but to serve as slaves of the gods and of their earthly regents. The tasks of humanity are to till the soil, to produce foods for sacrifice to the gods (represented by the king and the priestly caste), to build the sacred city Babylon, and to fight and, if necessary, die in the king's wars. Such a myth reflects a highly centralized state in which the king rules as Marduk's representative on earth. Resistance to the king is treason against the gods. Unquestioning obedience is the highest virtue, and order the highest religious value.

In their ritual the Babylonians reenacted the original battle by which world order was won and chaos subdued. This victory was celebrated liturgically in the New Year's festival, when the king ceremonially played the part of Marduk, reasserting that victory and staving off for another year the dreaded reversion of all things into formlessness and disorder.

This ritual is not only cultic, therefore, but military. As Marduk's representative on earth, the king has as his task to subdue all those enemies who threaten the tranquillity that he has established on behalf of the god. The whole cosmos is a state, and the god rules through the king. Politics arises within the divine sphere itself. Salvation *is* politics: identifying with the god of order against the god of chaos, and offering oneself up for the holy war required to impose order and rule on the peoples round about. And because chaos threatens repeatedly, in the form of barbarian attacks, an ever-expanding imperial policy is the automatic correlate of Marduk's ascendancy over all the gods.

The ultimate outcome of this type of myth, remarks Ricoeur, is a theology of war founded on the identification of the enemy with the powers that the god has vanquished and continues to vanquish in the drama of creation. Every coherent theology of holy war ultimately reverts to this basic mythological type. Unlike the biblical myth, which sees evil as an intrusion into a good creation and war as a consequence of the fall, this myth regards war as present from the beginning.

The Babylonian creation story is thus a myth about the redemptive power of violence. The distinctive feature of the myth is the victory of order over chaos by means of violence. This myth is the original religion of the status quo, the first articulation of "might makes right." It is the basic ideology of the Domination System. The gods favor those who conquer. Conversely, whoever conquers must have the favor of the gods. The mass of people exists to perpetuate the power and privilege that the gods have conferred on the rulers. Religion exists to legitimate power and privilege. Life is combat. Any form of order is preferable to chaos, according to this myth. Ours is neither a perfect nor a perfectible world; it is a theater of perpetual conflict in which the prize goes to the strong. Peace through war; security through strength: These are the core convictions that arise from this ancient historical religion.

This myth also inadvertently reveals the price men have paid for the power they acquired over women: complete servitude to their earthly rulers and heavenly gods. Women for their part were identified with inertia, chaos, and anarchy. Now "Woman is to man as nature is to culture"—the ideology that rationalizes the subordination of women in patriarchal societies by presenting it as if it were a universal reality.

This primordial myth is far from finished. It is as universally present and earnestly believed today as at any time in its long and bloody history. It is the dominant myth in contemporary America, more influential by far than Judaism or Christianity. It enshrines a cult of violence at the very heart of public life, and even those who seek to oppose its oppressive violence often do so using the very same means. It is the basis of foreign policy, nationalism, the cold war, militarism, the media, and televangelism. But its simplest, most pervasive, and finally most influential form, where it captures the imaginations of each new generation, is children's comics, cartoon shows, video games, and movies.

Here is how the myth of redemptive violence structures the standard comic strip or television cartoon sequence. An indestructible good guy is unalterably opposed to an irreformable and equally indestructible bad guy. Nothing can kill the good guy, although for the first three-quarters of the strip or show he (rarely she) suffers grievously, appearing hopelessly trapped, until somehow the hero breaks free, vanquishes the villain, and restores order until the next installment. Nothing finally destroys the bad guy or prevents his reappearance, whether he is soundly trounced, jailed, drowned, or shot into outer space.

Only the names have changed. Marduk subdues Tiamat through violence, and although he kills Tiamat, chaos incessantly reasserts itself, and is kept at bay only by repeated battles and by the repetition of the New Year's festival, where the heavenly combat myth is ritually reenacted. The structure of the combat myth is thus faithfully repeated on television week after week: A superior force representing chaos launches an aggressive attack; the champion fights back; the hero defeats the evil power decisively and reaffirms order over chaos. Willis Elliott's observation underscores the seriousness of this entertainment: "Cosmogony [the birth of the world] is egogony [the birth of the individual]: you are being birthed through how you see 'all things' as being birthed." Therefore, *"Whoever controls the cosmogony controls the children."*

The psychodynamics of the TV cartoon or comic book are marvelously simple: Children identify with the good guy so that they can think of themselves as good. This enables them to project onto the bad guy their own repressed anger, violence, rebelliousness, or lust, and then vicariously to enjoy their own evil by watching the bad guy initially prevail. (This segment of the show actually consumes all but the closing minutes, allowing ample time for indulging the dark side of the self.) When the good guy finally wins, viewers are then able to reassert control over their own inner tendencies, repress them, and reestablish a sense of goodness. Salvation is guaranteed through identification with the hero.

This structure cannot be altered. The villain does not simply lose more often, he must always lose. Otherwise, this entire view of reality would collapse. The good guys must always win. In order to suppress the fear of erupting chaos, the same mythic pattern must be endlessly repeated in myriad variations that never in any way alter the basic structure.

How is it possible that this ancient archetypal structure still possesses such power in a modern, secular, scientific culture? Thanks to the American penchant for letting viewer interest determine programming, the story lines of cartoons, television shows, comics, and movies tend to gravitate to the lowest common denominator of mythic simplicity. The head of programming at a major network was asked to describe the thinking process that led to the network's selection of programs. He answered: There was no thinking process whatsoever. TV and film producers provide whatever fare the ratings and box offices tell them will generate the most immediate profit. With important exceptions, the entertainment industry does not create materials that will be good for children to watch—material that will inculcate high values, ethical standards, honesty, truthfulness, mutual care and consideration, responsibility, and nobility of character. Instead, what children themselves prefer determines what is produced. The myth of redemptive violence is the simplest, laziest, most exciting, uncomplicated, irrational, and primitive depiction of evil the world has ever known.

Furthermore, its orientation toward evil is one *into which virtually all modern children (boys especially) are socialized in the process of maturation.* The myth that lay like a threshold across the path of burgeoning empires also lies across the path of each individual bred in such societies. Children select this mythic structure because they have already been led, by culturally reinforced cues and role models, to resonate with its simplistic view of reality. Its ubiquity is not the result of a conspiracy of Babylonian priests secretly buying up the mass media with Iraqi oil money, but a function of inculcated values endlessly reinforced by the Domination System.

Once children have been indoctrinated into the expectations of a dominator society, they may never outgrow the need to locate all evil outside themselves. Even as adults they tend to scapegoat others (the Commies, the Americans, the gays, the straights, the blacks, the whites) for all that is wrong in the world. They continue to depend on group identification and the upholding of social norms for a sense of well-being. There is a ritual dimension to television violence, involving the public in a reaffirmation of group values` through the ritualization of collective ideas.

In a period when Christian Sunday schools are dwindling, the myth of redemptive violence has won children's voluntary acquiescence to a regimen of religious indoctrination more exhaustive and effective than any in the history of religions. Estimates vary widely, but the average child is reported to log roughly thirty-six thousand hours of television by age eighteen, including some fifteen thousand murders. What church or synagogue can even remotely match the myth of redemptive violence in hours spent with children or quality of presentation? (Think of the typical "children's sermon"—how bland by comparison!)

No other religious system has ever remotely rivaled the myth of redemptive violence in its ability to catechize its young so totally. From the earliest age children are awash in depictions of violence as the ultimate solution in human conflicts. Nor does saturation in the myth end with the close of adolescence. There is no rite of passage from adolescent to adult status in the national cult of violence, but rather a years-long acclimatization to adult television and movie fare. Not all shows for children or adults are based on violence, of course. Reality is far more complex than the simplicities of this myth, and maturer minds will demand more subtle, nuanced, complex presentations. But the basic structure of the combat myth underlies the pap to which a great many adults turn in order to escape the harsher realities of their everyday lives: spy thrillers, westerns, cop shows, and combat programs. It is as if we must watch so much "redemptive" violence to reassure ourselves, against the deluge of facts to the contrary in our actual day-to-day lives, that reality really is that simple.

The structure of the ancient combat myth is not just the basis of comics and cartoons, however; it is the framework of much that passes as foreign policy. Subdue Tiamat, the argument runs, and a new world order will prevail. Holy wars, just wars, wars of national interest—all are legitimated by the appeal to the necessity of violence, the redemptive power of violence, the divine approval of violence. Christians have fallen headlong into reliance on violence. The nonviolent teaching of Jesus has been ignored. The strange new power of the cross, and Jesus' breaking of the spiral of violence, has been abandoned. Therefore the meaning of resurrection has been suppressed.

For if violence can save us, we do not need a redeemer. If violence is redemptive, Jesus' way of redeeming us is irrelevant. If we can produce salvation with military force, then we have no need for resurrection.

How odd that so many Christians have abandoned the creation story of Genesis 1 for a countermyth destructive of everything the Genesis story represents.

SECOND LESSON: GENESIS 22:1-18

Right at the fountainhead of Israel's unique history we begin to get the corrective to the myth of redemptive violence. God orders Abraham to sacrifice his only son, his beloved son, Isaac, the sole heir of the promises. Gods had not always demanded the sacrifice of firstborn sons; there had been a gentler period before the rise of the conquest states when the Goddess ruled human hearts, and the notion of placating remote and violent deities was apparently unknown. But the invention of warfare, patriarchy, ranking, and stratification in a society organized to benefit the few at the expense of the many brought with it new visions of the divine: male, ruthless, violent, nationalistic, bent on supremacy over all other gods. Such gods demanded to be appeased by the offering of what was most precious in the eyes of their subjects. Patriarchy had decreed the eldest son to be heir and family sovereign. Therefore the gods demanded, as occasion warranted, their devotees' most precious sons.

In his plodding obedience, in his willingness to comply with divine fiat, Abraham does nothing exceptional. Not one word of the text describes his emotions. We are not told that he acted with a heavy heart, or that he went wild with excitement when his son was spared, or that he even thanked God. He was simply doing his duty. He was obedient, and obedience, in a hierarchical social order, is the highest good. It is not Abraham that changes, not Abraham that rebels against an inhuman directive by a demonic god. It is God who changes. Or shall we be more delicate and suggest that God reveals God's true nature here? Either way, a major breakthrough: The myth of redemptive violence, which had spawned religions of sacral violence, has been repudiated by the divine itself. God begins to act more like a loving father, who one day would himself have a son, an only son whom he loved, a beloved son, who would also be taken up a mount. Only this time the knife would not be withheld. Now the God's great father's heart would break, and darkness devour the earth. God had finally learned to be nonviolent, but not God's children.

THIRD LESSON: EXODUS 14:10—15:1

When the new arrives, we have no categories for understanding it, so we try to squeeze it into the categories we already have. God had spared Isaac, and later Joseph. These made great stories, but what was the point? You do not change the whole structure of thought on the basis of a few anomalous narratives. God was already beginning to reveal to Israel the utter incompatibility of domination and divine love. But this was a people inured to violence like other peoples. It was not easy to recognize in these flashes of pure revelation that a whole new order was breaking into the world. God had told them as much; the election of Israel itself was the beginning of a new people of God, a light to the nations. But it was all too easy to hear "You are elected to be the bearer of this new light to all peoples" as "You are my special people and I love you more than all others." So the revelation was domesticated, pigeonholed into old categories, and neutralized.

But then Israel found itself enslaved in Egypt. And God delivered them. They did not lift a finger in their own defense. They did not achieve independence and liberation by means of a slave revolt or armed revolution. They did not learn war. It was not by means of their own cleverness or ruthlessness that they were now freed, but the sheer unmerited grace of a God whom they had not known before: I AM. Nor did God smite the Egyptians with heavenly armies, but through a synchronous natural event: a strong east wind that blew back the waters over the shallows and that ceased after the Israelites had made their crossing. Deadly, yes. But God had found a way to do it without teaching Israel war.

Even then, many of the Israelites resisted what God was doing. They said to Moses, "What have you done to us, bringing us out of Egypt? Is this not the very thing we told you in Egypt, 'Let us alone and let us serve the Egyptians'? For it would have been better for us to serve the Egyptians than to die in the wilderness." How deeply the myth of redemptive violence had sunk its talons into their psyches; here the slave demanded to be restored to slavery, to serve those whom the gods had ordained as their masters. The risks of freedom were too great; leave us alone. One of the great mysteries of domination is how it can be so deeply internalized that outer constraints and sanctions are scarcely necessary to keep the victims in line.

So revelation will not be enough. God must find a way to get the domination mentality out of people's souls. God's mighty acts in history will not be enough; there must be therapies and spiritual disciplines capable of tearing out those talons, binding up the wounds, and helping people through recurrent relapses. A popular saying of the 1960s ran, "The hardest battle isn't with Mr. Charlie. It's with what Mr. Charlie has done to your mind." But there can be no question here of simply healing people in order to return them to life in a system that is itself alienated and alienating. As a friend of mine put it, we need to stop trying to fix up people so that the system works better and to start fixing up the system so that people work better.

The task of Israel was to try to fashion a social system in which God's emergent new order would begin to become operational. That they failed in large measure should surprise no one; the church has failed equally. What alone matters is that, gradually, humanity is beginning to grasp the revelation. In the last 150 years we have witnessed the end of slavery, the birth of women's liberation, the struggle against racism and for civil rights, the exposure of human rights abuses, the emergence of the gay/lesbian rights movement, the explosive growth of the environmental movement, the rise in the number of democracies, the exposure of sexual and physical abuse of children, and the internationalization of moral outrage (as in the divestment campaign against South Africa). Each of these has provoked a massive recoil of resistance and conflict. If anything, these struggles have increased the total level of conflict in the world. But that inevitable fact must not blind us to the enormity of what is happening: The revelation is being perceived by increasing numbers of people. It is becoming harder and harder to convince people that domination is right. More and more people are questioning the morality of violence. People may not believe in the God revealed in the exodus and by Jesus, but they are increasingly certain that no god legitimates the oppression of some by others. And their unbelief in the Judeo-Christian God may be the consequence of our failure to grasp the central revelation and hold it before the world. We, too, have been deluded by the myth of redemptive violence, with our "just" wars and our trust in weaponry. But that will change. Nothing can stop this revelation from reaching its full course. The Word of God will not return empty.

FOURTH LESSON: ISAIAH 55:1-11

We cannot comprehend the pure graciousness of God's ways. The Israelites were not delivered from slavery because they were a superior race or a special people. God's concerted attack on domination is not a consequence of our deserving. However much we may rightly think of God as within us, there is an irreducible externality to grace that cannot be overlooked. It comes to us riding in the back of a pickup truck on the way to a fishing hole or at a meeting of Alcoholics Anonymous. It slams us to the ground on the way to kill a bunch of Christians or steals on us tenderly through a chorus from Handel's *Messiah.* We are going about our lives, perhaps even obsessively, not in the least open to God, when suddenly God is there.

Grace is not limited to the personal, however. It also occurs in the great sea-changes of history. We ourselves witnessed in 1989 nonviolent revolutions in thirteen nations comprising a third of the world's population, and all succeeded except in China. Did you notice *that* burning bush? Are we unable to name such miraculous events "the mighty acts of God"? If events on such a scale, unprecedented in all of human history, are not enough to convince us that they are of God, what would?

Grace can come unexpectedly, but we can also ask for it. It comes to those who are not even looking for it, but it comes also to those whose entire life is a focused hunger for God. Thus Isaiah cries out to the exiles, "Ho, everyone who thirsts, come to the waters; and you that have no money, come, buy and eat! Come, buy wine and milk without money and without price." To these, who have misdirected their life's energies "for that which is not bread," and their labor "for that which does not satisfy," God offers a covenant that will, amazingly, draw nations from the ends of the earth to tiny Israel, for nowhere else is the revelation made known that can end the nations' warfare. This God offers a clean start so wondrous it can scarcely be believed.

My wife and I recently did a workshop in a maximum security prison. Most of our group were lifers; many of them had killed. They were studying for the master of divinity degree. Each one of these men was an incomprehensible miracle. God had found them in the hellish conditions of our prisons, and grace had turned their lives around. There could be no question of making it up to society; the dead could not be brought back to life. Yet God had penetrated their hearts and given them a new start.

It is not easy to find God in a society organized to suppress even the hint of powers or realities transcending the powers exercised by the ruling authorities. God can find us nonetheless. But sometimes it takes a horrific blow to waken us from our mesmerized sleep. One prisoner told us that incarceration was the best thing that ever happened to him. He did not mean that lightly. It in no way excuses the brutality of our prison system. But he had killed a man in a drunken brawl, and prison life had shocked him into admitting his alcoholism and into getting help. God had found him in the depths and had given him new life, "without money and without price."

FIFTH LESSON: ROMANS 6:3-11

We surely know already the power of the resurrection. Whenever a life is transformed or justice is done or we experience the ineffable presence of God, we already know resurrection. Resurrection is not something that happens to us when we die and go to heaven; it is a quality of living that we enter into the moment we are reconnected with God. It is not simply immortality after death (which, as William Stringfellow once remarked, is merely an elaborate synonym for memory), although it is certainly true that everything we are and have done is gathered up into God for all eternity, so that nothing shall be lost. Resurrection is a dimension of being in which we live and move and have our being already, in this life. Resurrection, Stringfellow continues, is living in emancipation from the power of death. It is participation in a moral universe; it is the temporal fulfillment of life. Heaven is no more a site in the galaxies than hell is located in the bowels of the earth. To surrender this world to the powers of death and seek fulfillment in an afterlife is the final abdication to the power of death (*An Ethic for Christians and Other Aliens in a Strange Land* [Waco: Word Books, 1973]).

But resurrection, as Paul makes clear, is not just what happens on this earth. Once we enter eternity, we continue in eternity for all eternity. In his brilliant discussion in Romans 6, Paul deliberately avoids the equation, Christ was raised, we are raised. Instead, he insists, we *will be raised,* we *will also live with him,* we *will be united with him in a resurrection like his.* We are already raised to newness of life, no longer enslaved to sin, alive to God in Christ Jesus. We have the firstfruits of eternal life. We have a foretaste of it. We are already united with Christ. But not fully. However powerful our experiences of resurrection in this life, they are given under the conditions of the old order. We are still hemmed in by finitude, habitual reactions, deep explosive eruptions of our shadow side, and words and acts that damage ourselves and others. We are still unable to live without collusion with the Domination System, however much we try. So we live between the already of redemption and the not yet of total restoration.

Resurrection is the guarantee, down payment, and hope that the new order of God that is coming will ultimately prevail over the Domination System. It is the affirmation that every death offered to further that new order is meaningful, gathered up into the loving heart of God. But it is finally unimaginable and unthinkable, and attempts to describe it trespass on mystery. Truth is, all we know about resurrection is what we have already experienced of the reality of God. And that is most certainly enough.

GOSPEL: MARK 16:1-8; MATTHEW 28:1-10

Mark's account, unlike Matthew's (where Jesus appears to the women on their way to tell the disciples about the empty tomb), is not a resurrection narrative at all. Indeed, if Mark's Gospel did in fact end at verse 8, Mark contains no resurrection narrative, just an ambiguous empty tomb. And women who are too terrified to tell even about it. It is a strange way to end a Gospel. Almost as an afterthought, the narrator says, By the way, some women went to the tomb but found it empty, except for an angel (or young man) who left them a message.

The other Gospels make up for Mark's brevity. But they themselves do not agree even in a single duplicate account. Something surpassingly strange is going on here. If the early church had been in the business of creating resurrection stories in order to edify the faithful and snow the gullible, they would surely have followed the example of Paul, who lists not one single woman witness of the resurrection (1 Cor. 15:3-8). Women had no standing as witnesses in Judaism. Yet all four Gospels portray women at the empty tomb. And Matthew and John show Jesus appearing first to the women. Later evidence documents the embarrassment the church felt over the prominence given women in a matter supremely necessitating valid and credible witnesses. It is tempting to say that God has a great sense of humor.

But more is at stake here than God's fierce whimsy. The witnesses of Jesus' birth in Luke had been shepherds, known to be notorious liars and poachers, and therefore also disallowed as witnesses. So at the beginning and end of the story, we are presented with marginalized people, invalid witnesses, and are asked to believe the preposterous.

The issue here is not historical, however. It is a matter of believing not whether Jesus' resurrection really happened but whether God is really like that. The issue is not whether Jesus' body was gathered up to heaven but whether it is really true that God has now sided with the people on the edges and at the bottom. What the early hearers of the story (who couldn't have cared less about historicity) understood was that God had turned the world upside down, transvaluing all the corrupt values of the Domination System. The reason people flocked to the early church was not that they believed the resurrection story (remember, Mark doesn't even feel it necessary to tell such stories) but that they heard in the Gospel story the unbelievably wonderful news that God was now ending patriarchy, ranking, hierarchicalism, ethnic superiority, empire building, and the religion of sacral violence. They heard that women were as good as men, that sinners were as welcome as saints, that poor were as worthy as rich.

Yes, the Powers killed Jesus, but he wouldn't stay dead. He had unleashed a revolution that would transform the world down to its very structures. He was alive in all the people who had reclaimed their human dignity, all those who had accepted God's forgiveness, all those who had been healed of their diseases or freed from demonic possession. Those who had once abandoned themselves to making do in a wrong order had now stood up and claimed God's domination-free order and were living as if it had already come. They knew Christ and the power of his resurrection (Phil. 3:10). Resurrection is the promise that the new order will finally come, but it is also the possibility of living resurrection existence in the midst of domination and violence here and now.

So it was no problem to "believe in" the resurrection. The early Christians were experiencing it in the immediacy of God's presence. They could see it in people's changed lives. They understood it as the presence of life in a world sold out to death. Resurrection was the banner they unfurled as they went out to meet domination in all its forms. "Believing in" the resurrection is a modern and quite bogus problem, created by our fascination with historicity. We want to know if it could have been filmed. It is not intrinsic implausibility that makes it so hard for us to believe; after all, the new physics keeps uncovering a universe that seems weirder and weirder. It is our enslavement to the doctrines of materialism, historical positivism, and a narrow-minded rationalism that make belief difficult.

The early Christians had no such problem. And I suppose we should not either, if we *know* the living God, if we have experienced what it means to pass from death to life, if we have been crucified with Christ to the Domination System ("this world"). Then, over us, too, death will have no dominion (Rom. 6:9). For resurrection is, finally, utter trust that God is in charge of this universe, that it is very, very good, and that all things shall be good, and better than good, unimaginably good, when the kingdom of this world becomes the kingdom of our God and of God's Christ.